I0763178
THIS BELONGS TO

YESTERDAY TODAY & TOMORROW

A Daily Guide to
Reflect, Grow, and Dream

This edition published by Piccadilly (USA) Inc.

10 9 8 7 6 5 4 3 2 1

Made in China

ISBN: 978-1-48897-520-2

Welcome to **"Yesterday, Today, & Tomorrow: A Daily Guide to Reflect, Grow & Dream."** This reflection tool is a companion on your journey through time, offering a space for introspection, contemplation, and exploration. Each writing prompt presents an opportunity to traverse the reflections of yesterday, embrace the experiences of today, and envision the dreams of tomorrow.

These pages offer the mindful practice of writing through self-discovery. It will challenge you to reflect on the growth you've had from past experiences while simultaneously reflecting on your present transformation and outlook. This process dares you to examine how you will continue to evolve in the future and view your life from a completely different perspective.

First, we will guide you with inspiration from a quote, word, song lyric, idea, invention, piece of pop culture history, or an excerpt from a poem. Then, we will provide a three-part writing prompt for each idea. The three parts for each prompt will consist of yesterday, today, and tomorrow.

For the "yesterday" prompt, you will reflect on a memory or part of your life from your past. In the "today" prompt, focus on your present—the here and now. Finally, in the "tomorrow" prompt, contemplate your future and what has yet to come. Give each prompt thoughtful consideration and delve deeply into what has been, what is, and what will be. Allow yourself to shape your future through your journey, drawing lessons from yesterday and today. Appreciate fondly all the moments that have made up your life, and exuberantly anticipate the moments that you will make.

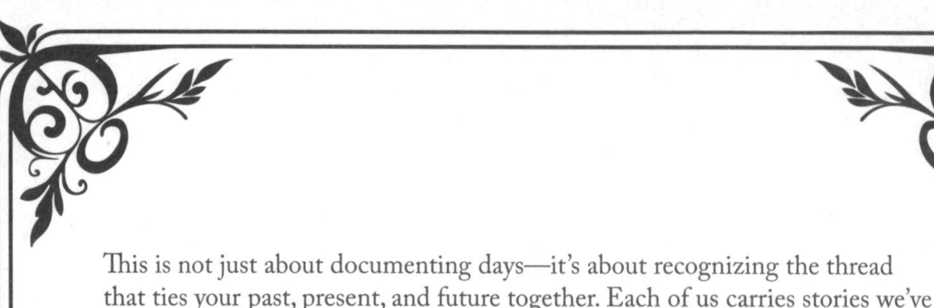

This is not just about documenting days—it's about recognizing the thread that ties your past, present, and future together. Each of us carries stories we've lived, stories we're living, and stories we're still writing. Through this process, you may begin to notice recurring themes, unexpected patterns, or quiet truths that have always been waiting beneath the surface.

Let this guide be a place where time bends—not in a rush to move forward, but in a moment-to-moment celebration of who you've been, who you are, and who you are becoming. Growth isn't always loud. Sometimes it whispers through memory, decision, or hope. This journey invites all of it.

You don't need to know where you're going to begin. All you need is a willingness to show up with honesty. There is no right answer, no perfect way to reflect. Let your pen follow where your thoughts wander, and trust that something meaningful will always rise from the process.

"WE ARE NOT JUST THE STORIES WE TELL OURSELVES, BUT ALSO THE ONES WE ARE WILLING TO REWRITE."

— Brené Brown

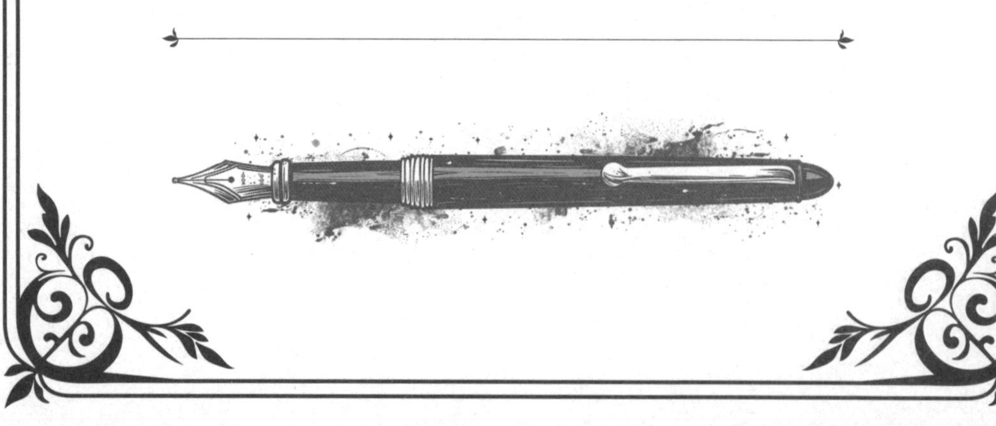

"THE PAST"

The past and present with me ever stand,

Their shadows lengthen on the quiet land.

The joys I knew, the tears I could not stay,

Are folded now within the light of day.

I walk with both, a hand in either hand,

And find my way through all life's shifting sand.

by Henry Wadsworth Longfellow

STARTING EXERCISE: MAPPING YOUR TIME THREADS

Before you begin your journey through the prompts, take time to ground yourself in your own story. This exercise helps you reflect on the emotional tone, meaningful events, and lingering questions that have shaped your past, define your present, and influence your future. This simple map will act as a foundation—revealing the themes and thoughts you may return to as you move forward.

On the following pages you will see three columns titled **Yesterday, Today, and Tomorrow**. In each column, complete the following:

1 Three Words That Describe How You Felt During That Time

For **Yesterday,** choose three words that capture how you felt during a specific period of your past (childhood, adolescence, a pivotal chapter, etc.). Think about the emotional tone of that time.

For **Today**, choose three words that describe how you feel in your life right now.

For **Tomorrow,** choose three words that describe how you imagine or hope to feel in the future.

Examples: hopeful, lost, overwhelmed, excited, invisible, brave.

2 Three Moments or Themes That Stand Out

For each timeframe, think about the defining memories, patterns, or recurring experiences. These might be emotional milestones, roles you played, personal discoveries, or habits you've noticed.

Examples:

Yesterday: "Moving to a new town," "Trying to fit in," "A feeling of being misunderstood."

Today: "Learning to set boundaries," "Reconnecting with creativity," "Uncertainty in career."

Tomorrow: "Starting over with intention," "Finding peace in solitude," "Letting go of fear."

3 One Question You're Still Holding from That Period of Your Life

Reflect on a question that still lingers from each stage. This might be something unresolved, something you're still curious about, or something you're still learning to understand.

Examples:

Yesterday: "Why did I feel like I had to hide parts of myself?"

Today: "What does it really mean to feel content?"

Tomorrow: "Will I be brave enough to become who I want to be?"

Time

YESTERDAY	TODAY	TOMORROW
1	1	1
2	2	2
3	3	3

We've all heard the saying at one point in our lives "Don't judge a book by its cover." Which is a good reminder of acceptance and the benefit of not making assumptions.

YESTERDAY: What assumptions in the past have you made about someone that turned out to be completely wrong? How did you feel prematurely judging them?

TODAY: What do people usually assume about you that turns out to be incorrect? Why do you think they have these preconceived notions about you?

TOMORROW: Looking forward what do you hope people overlook (don't judge) about you, what do you want them to see instead?

Molière once said, 'The greater the obstacle, the more glory in overcoming it! Each challenge we face is an opportunity to build resilience and discover our true potential.

YESTERDAY: Recall a moment when you faced a daunting challenge. How did you feel, and what hidden strengths did you uncover in the process of overcoming it?

TODAY: Consider a current challenge. How is it shaping your daily thoughts and actions, and what does this reveal about your personal growth?

TOMORROW: Envision a future challenge. How might you approach it with the wisdom you've accumulated, and what new strengths or insights do you hope to gain?

Pulitzer Prize poet Mary Oliver understood the value of life when she wrote, "Tell me, what is it you plan to do with your one wild and precious life?"

YESTERDAY: Looking back what do you remember were the earliest plans you made for your life? What were your very first hopes, dreams, and aspirations?

TODAY: Thinking about the present how have your plans changed for your life from your younger years until now? What was the turning point that moved you in a different direction?

TOMORROW: Fast forward to your future and you've lived much of your life, when you look back what do you hope your life will look like? What do you think will have made your life fulfilled?

The song "Time" by Pink Floyd, centers around how time is valuable but fleeting and laments about how one day you'll wish you had all the time back you wasted.. These lyrics capture their sentiment best, "Ticking away the moments that make up a dull day. You fritter and waste the hours in an offhand way. Kicking around on a piece of ground in your hometown, waiting for someone or something to show you the way."

YESTERDAY: Turn the clock back and think about your past, did you value your time back then, or did you waste it? What struggles did you face when it came to managing your time wisely?

TODAY: Do you look at time differently now that you're older and if so, what has changed? How old were you when you realized how valuable time is?

TOMORROW: If you skip ahead to your future, how do you want to spend your time and will you allow yourself to waste time on anything? Why or why not?

Downtown Abbey gave the world six seasons of pure dramatic entertainment. No doubt some of the show's wisdom will live on throughout history like when Isobel Crowley shared this good advice, "Seems a pity not to take a chance to end a quarrel. Isn't it better than to let it fester?"

YESTERDAY: Recall the first time you fought with a friend. What started it, what happened and how did things end? How did that experience leave you feeling?

TODAY: Do you handle arguments or quarrels differently than you did when you were younger? If so, what's the main difference, and what contributed to this change?

TOMORROW: Thinking ahead to a time when you're much older, what do you hope you will not have to fight about anymore? Do you have any unresolved grudges from past disagreements with others you hope to work out? Explain.

Playwright George Bernard Shaw encourages a proactive approach to life with his statement, "Don't wait for the right opportunity; create it." Shaw's words inspire individuals to take initiative, and not to rely solely on external circumstances but actively shaping their opportunities.

YESTERDAY: Regarding your past was there any opportunity you regret not capitalizing on? Describe the situation and elaborate on how this experience has altered your perspective on opportunities.

TODAY: Have you recently created any opportunities for yourself? If so, what were the results of your efforts?

TOMORROW: As you contemplate the future, what ambitions or goals are you envisioning? Reflect on the opportunities you aspire to create, not only for yourself but also for those around you.

Bob Goff imparts a valuable perspective with his quote, "Embrace uncertainty. Some of the most beautiful chapters in our lives won't have a title until much later." Goff's words inspire a sense of openness to the unpredictable and a recognition that the most meaningful moments often reveal themselves in due course.

YESTERDAY: Thinking back towards your early years, how would you describe the first few chapters of your life? What was the biggest uncertainty you faced that you wish you would have embraced?

TODAY: If you were going to start writing a memoir today, what would be the main topic you focus on regarding your current life? Are you still struggling with uncertainty and if so, what specifically?

TOMORROW: Considering Bob Goff's quote about the beauty of chapters unfolding later, what do you hope those chapters will be filled with?

The mantra 'Live, Laugh, Love' emerged as one of the most inspirational sayings of the 21st century, swiftly transcending its origin to grace motivational posters, art, and home décor worldwide.

YESTERDAY: Jump back in time and apply this phrase (live, laugh, love) to your past. What did it look like?

TODAY: Describe how you live currently, what makes you laugh, and who or what do you love? How has this changed through the years?

TOMORROW: Think about yourself in the years to come and how you'll have grown, what do you want this phrase to represent in your future?

There's a timeless cautionary saying that warns us, 'Be careful who you trust. Salt and sugar look the same.' This metaphor serves as a reminder to exercise caution in judging the true nature of individuals.

YESTERDAY: Recall your first experience where someone broke your trust or betrayed you. How did that change you and what did it teach you?

TODAY: Taking what you've learned about trust through time, how do you handle situations today when the ability to trust someone comes into question? What do you do now you didn't back then?

TOMORROW: Looking ahead is there someone you hope to trust again, or do you hope to trust yourself again in a way? Explain.

Buddha's profound words serve as a gentle reminder of the importance of living in the moment: 'The past is already gone; the future is not yet here. There's only one moment for you to live.'"

YESTERDAY: Do you dwell on your past too much? Are you living in the rearview mirror, or do you just revisit from time to time? Describe your relationship with your yesterdays.

TODAY: It's beneficial to live in the moment, and enjoy the present and all that is happening around you. Do you struggle with being present and if so, why?

TOMORROW: Does the future make you excited, apprehensive or uncertain? Write about your emotions and use an analogy to describe your feelings.

There's a popular English proverb parents have been teaching their children for centuries that states: two wrongs don't make a right.

YESTERDAY: In your past when someone wronged you, how did you handle it?

TODAY: Thinking about this proverb in the present tense, how do you handle it when someone wrongs you today? How has your view on retaliation or reaction changed over the years and is that a testament to your emotional maturity?

TOMORROW: If you have kids or grandchildren and they come to you with a problem where they've been wronged, what will you say to them? What good examples from your life will you use?

"Somewhere, over the rainbow, skies are blue, and the dreams that you dare to dream really do come true," those are just part of the lyrics from the signature song Somewhere Over the Rainbow, from *The Wizard of Oz* soundtrack. For generations, it has inspired people to dare to dream.

YESTERDAY: Looking ahead to what's to come, do you think you will ever stop dreaming once you achieve your current goals, or will you continue to dream until the end of your days? What was the feeling like when you experienced it?

TODAY: What are your current hopes and dreams and what steps are you taking to make them come true?

TOMORROW: Thinking forward to what's to come do you think you will ever stop dreaming if you reach your current goals or will you dream until the end of your days?

"The belief that you can have a meaningful career is the first step to finding one," is a direct quote from Sean Aiken who created *The One Week Job Project*. He worked 52 jobs in 52 weeks to find his passion. This idea came to Aiken when he realized he was unsure of what career to pursue after obtaining a business degree.

YESTERDAY: What did you want your career to be when you were younger and how did that change as you got older?

TODAY: What is your current career? How did you end up where you are today as opposed to what you wanted back then, and how do you feel about it?

TOMORROW: Will there be any future career changes and if so, what inspired the change? What will this change fulfill that your current career doesn't?

During a peculiar exchange in Lewis Carroll's *Alice's Adventures in Wonderland*, the Caterpillar questions Alice, asking, 'Who are you?' To which Alice replies, rather shyly, 'I–I hardly know, sir, just at present—at least I know who I was when I got up this morning, but I think I must have been changed several times since then.'

YESTERDAY: Our youth is a time for exploring ourselves and who we want to become. Describe your journey and what you discovered about yourself.

TODAY: How are you a different person today than the person you were yesterday?

TOMORROW: Looking ahead to when you're older than you are today (some years down the road) what changes do you think will have happened by then? Is there a specific personal growth you hope to achieve by then?

Most people have heard the motto 'Go big or go home,' and many have even used it themselves. This phrase signifies the importance of giving your all and holding nothing back.

YESTERDAY: When you were younger think about a time when you "went big" and what motivated you to do so? Did this lay the foundation for you to give it all you got every time you try something?

TODAY: How does this motto apply to your life today or have you adopted a new mindset? Explain.

TOMORROW: Thinking ahead if you had to apply this phrase to something in the future, what do you think it would be and why?

One of Warner Bros.' most beloved cartoons is *Looney Tunes*, largely attributed to the timeless charm of Bugs Bunny. In the famous episode 'A-Lad-In His Lamp,' the plot revolves around a Genie who grants wishes but proves to be a tricky manipulator. However, his schemes meet their match in the quick-witted rabbit.

YESTERDAY: If you could make a wish to return to a specific time or event in your life, which would you choose, and why do you want to revisit that moment?

TODAY: If you were given a wish to be granted right now, what would you wish for?

TOMORROW: If you were granted three wishes for your future, with the condition that none of them could involve material possessions, what would you wish for?

The Dalai Lama created a list titled 'Instructions for Life,' similar to a user manual for mankind, and one of its principles emphasizes the importance of opening your arms to change while steadfastly holding onto your values.

YESTERDAY: What was the first big change you had to make in your life and how did you navigate it? What was the hardest part?

TODAY: How would you describe your current values and which value is non-negotiable when it comes to change?

TOMORROW: Thinking about your days ahead do you foresee a time when you may have to make a change that could challenge your virtues or values? What do you think you'll do when faced with this scenario?

Carpe diem is Latin for "seize the day" and has been a widely used phrase to inspire people to make the most of the day they've been given.

YESTERDAY: Looking back at your past, what did a typical day look like, and did you ever think about seizing the day? When was the first time you heard this phrase?

TODAY: What does your typical day look like currently? Do you feel like you make the most of your day – why or why not? Is there anything you'd like to do differently and if so, what's stopping you?

TOMORROW: When you get older, closer to retirement do you think you will continue to "seize the day" why or why not? How do you think your perspective will shift when you think about making the most of your day as time becomes more precious?

You've likely heard someone mention they were on the 'struggle bus,' indicating they were facing difficulty. It's never a pleasant ride, but we've all experienced those difficult moments.

YESTERDAY: Is there any part of your past you struggle with, something negative you don't like to think of? How can you change the way you see that – what strengths or lessons can you find from your past that made for a better today?

TODAY: What's the biggest struggle you're facing presently and what steps can you take, so that your future self can look back on this moment with a more positive light?

TOMORROW: When you look to the future what are you afraid you'll struggle with? What change is coming that will be hardest for you to acclimate to and why? Is there anything you can do now to prepare for it?

"That's the thing about pain, it demands to be felt," is a memorable excerpt from John Green's book, *The Fault in Our Stars*, which gained such popularity that it was adapted into a movie starring Shailene Woodley.

YESTERDAY: Recall a time from your past that was so painful you didn't know how you would get through it.

TODAY: Have you learned anything from past hurts that helps you process painful situations today – if so, what?

TOMORROW: When you envision your future, what painful scenarios do you hope to leave behind and resign to the past?

Athena Singh, through her quote, 'Never trust your fears - they don't know your strength,' reminds us that we have the capacity to overcome the things that scare us.

YESTERDAY: What scared you as a child and did you develop any phobias because of this fear?

TODAY: Thinking about today, do you still have those same fears, or have you outgrown them? Do you have any new fears you didn't have before?

TOMORROW: Do you have any fears concerning the future, all the tomorrows ahead of you – if so, what?

The term 'frenemy' has become widely used in pop culture, akin to the sentiment expressed by Michael Corleone in the movie *The Godfather: Part Two* released in 1974: "Keep your friends close, but your enemies closer."

YESTERDAY: Who was your first frenemy or rival and what caused the two of you to have this type of dynamic?

TODAY: What are your current thoughts on frenemies? Have you moved beyond this stage, or do you anticipate that there will always be someone with whom you have this kind of relationship?

TOMORROW: In the near future, do you anticipate moving beyond the need to watch out for enemies, or do you believe maintaining this mindset will continue to keep you on your toes?

The expression 'The grass is greener on the other side' was once a popular way for people to compare their situations with others, implying that they might be happier with what someone else had. However, the saying has been revised to convey a different perspective: "The grass isn't greener on the other side; it's greener where you water it."

YESTERDAY: Reflect on the first instance when you believed the grass was greener somewhere else and the reasons why you felt that way.

TODAY: Do you think you're watering the grass where you are right now or are you still daydreaming about the grass being greener elsewhere? Explain.

TOMORROW: As you contemplate your future, what steps can you take now to avoid looking back with regrets? Is there a current challenge, such as a lack of appreciation, boredom, or another factor that you need to address?

This Native American proverb beautifully captures the essence of personal growth: “The journey between who you once were and who you are now becoming is where the dance of life really takes place.” It personifies the transformative nature of the human experience.

YESTERDAY: Recall a time from your past when you went on a journey of self-discovery and what did you learn about yourself that shaped who you are today?

TODAY: Thinking about where you are now, describe how far you’ve come and what you’ve overcome to get to where you are today.

TOMORROW: As you look forward to your future, what do you hope to have figured out and experienced on your life’s journey? What actions are you currently taking to ensure those aspirations become a reality?

National Lampoon's Vacation is a family-friendly movie that chronicles the misadventures of the Griswold family during a cross-country vacation to an amusement park. Hijinks ensue as a dad, Clark Griswold, insists on making the journey in a station wagon, choosing family bonding over the convenience of flying.

YESTERDAY: Thinking about your childhood, describe your most memorable family vacation and what you learned about your family as a result.

TODAY: If you were to leave for a vacation right now, where would you choose to go, and what type of vacation would you love to experience?

TOMORROW: Drawing inspiration from the sentiment in National Lampoon's Vacation, where the focus is on family bonding, in the future when you plan a memorable family vacation, where would you go and what activities will you choose that will foster connection and create lasting memories?

Martin Luther King Jr. delivered one of the most popular and influential speeches in history, known as the 'I Have a Dream' speech. A poignant excerpt from this speech emphasizes the importance of righteousness on the path to gaining our rightful place: "In the process of gaining our rightful place, we must not be guilty of wrongful deeds. Let us not seek to satisfy our thirst for freedom by drinking from the cup of bitterness and hatred."

YESTERDAY: Looking back as you were growing up were you subjected to ostracism, bullying, or discrimination while attempting to fit in? Did these experiences ever provoke a desire to react negatively? How did you navigate and cope with such situations?

TODAY: Thinking about the present when someone or a situation makes you feel wronged what is your first instinct and how is that different from how you used to act? What eye-opening experience changed the way you respond?

TOMORROW: Fast forward years ahead what are you hopeful that you'll never have to deal with again that you were always confronted with in your past in terms of finding your place in this world?

Upon moving into a new house, Emily Dickinson penned one of her most poignant quotes to a friend: 'I am out with lanterns looking for myself.' In this reflection, she captured the essence of trying to find a sense of belonging in an unfamiliar place.

YESTERDAY: Reflecting on your childhood what do you remember made your house feel like home?

TODAY: Thinking about your life now, do you ever get homesick and if so, what is missing that makes you feel that way?

TOMORROW: Thinking ahead as you build your family what will you pass down to your children that will help them experience the same feeling of home you did as a child?

There's an old Irish blessing that echoes a meaningful reminder: 'May you never forget what is worth remembering, nor ever remember what is best forgotten.' It perfectly sums up a wish for a life filled with cherished memories and the wisdom to let go of those best left behind.

YESTERDAY: When reflecting on your past, what aspects do you believe are best forgotten, and what moments or lessons are worth remembering?

TODAY: Reflecting on your present, what aspects would you prefer to forget, and what moments do you anticipate remembering fondly?

TOMORROW: What memories you are eagerly looking forward to creating that bring excitement about the future? Explore the emotions, experiences, and moments that fill you with anticipation for what lies ahead.

The origin of the phrase "the world is your oyster" can be traced back to Shakespeare's play *The Merry Wives of Windsor*. In Act 2, Scene 2, the character Pistol declares, 'Why then the world's mine oyster, which I with sword will open.' This expression conveys the idea that the world is brimming with opportunities and possibilities, awaiting exploration.

YESTERDAY: As you were growing up what possibilities were you excited about exploring? Did you view the world as your oyster, why or why not?

TODAY: Thinking about your present day, how are you making the world your oyster? What opportunities are you making the most of and what possibilities are you exploring?

TOMORROW: Thinking about your future, what dreams have come true, and what opportunities made this possible?

The term "binge-watching" gained popularity through streaming services like Netflix. Oftentimes, as we immerse ourselves in TV series, we find snippets of our lives reflected in the narratives. Conversely, there are moments when we can't help but feel grateful for the life we have, especially when compared to the chaotic scenarios depicted in some sitcoms.

YESTERDAY: Imagine your past as a TV series trailer and pilot episode, offering glimpses of the years to come. Envision the scenes that will unfold, capturing the essence of your journey and setting the stage for the coming chapters of your life.

TODAY: Imagine your present-day as the third season of the TV series. The audience is engaged and invested in what is happening and what is yet to come.

TOMORROW: Look ahead to the series finale, what will happen in the last season of the TV series? What unanswered questions will be revealed, what broken fences have been mended, and what is next for the lead characters?

Frequently Asked Questions, or FAQs, play a crucial role in enhancing the customer experience on your website by providing answers to commonly asked questions about your product or service. This organized approach not only facilitates quick access to information but also contributes to customer satisfaction. If life offered a similar service, imagine the convenience of readily available answers to the most common queries.

YESTERDAY: What questions did you have growing up that you wished you had an FAQ source to turn to, and who did you go to with most of your questions?

TODAY: Share your current approach to handling questions or problems in your life now. What methods do you use to find the answers you need? Do you have someone you trust to turn to for valuable advice?

TOMORROW: Look ahead several years from now and think about when you are faced with problems that need answers. Will you use the same methods you do now? Consider the possibility of gaining newfound wisdom with age and whether this might lead to the adoption of different tactics for addressing problems in the future.

Slow and steady wins the race is an expression that has been uttered universally to emphasize the importance of consistency through progress even if it's slower as opposed to racing through things that lead to carelessness.

YESTERDAY: Think about a time in your past when something didn't progress as quickly as you wanted it to, and you ended up rushing which led to an unfortunate outcome.

TODAY: Thinking about where you are now in your life, what have you learned about progress and what is your philosophy on the matter?

TOMORROW: Looking ahead what progress do you hope to have made over the next 10 years and do you have a plan on how to get there?

The Neighborhood of Make-Believe is the fictional kingdom inhabited by puppet characters on the children's television series *Mr. Roger's Neighborhood.* Fred Rogers created his own world through his imagination.

YESTERDAY: How did you use your imagination as a child? What was the most creative thing you did when you were younger?

TODAY: Reflect on the role of your imagination presently. Have factors like societal influences, personal growth, and evolving perspectives changed the way you use your creativity? Delve into ways your imagination has shaped your experiences over time.

TOMORROW: As you get older do you worry you will lose the ability to be creative with your imagination? Do you think you will use it differently in the distant future and if so, how?

Karma is a concept present in numerous ancient cultures and religions. It is an action linked to the principle of cause and effect. Essentially, it operates on the boomerang principle; you reap what you sow.

YESTERDAY: Consider your past relationships and whether there's a specific instance where you believe someone has wronged you, prompting a desire that karma should intervene. How have these experiences shaped your views on fairness and consequences in relationships?

TODAY: Reflect on whether, at this stage, you embrace or question the principles of karma, and expand on the reasons behind your current outlook.

TOMORROW: Have your past actions given you concerns about karma impacting your future? Reflect on any instances throughout your life until now that make you apprehensive about potential visits from karma.

One of the Foo Fighters' most popular hits, 'My Hero,' serves as a tribute to everyday people. According to lead singer Dave Grohl, the song is an acknowledgment of his admiration for ordinary individuals who perform extraordinary deeds.

YESTERDAY: Thinking back to when you were younger, who do you remember being your first hero and what made them heroic in your eyes?

TODAY: Consider how your definition of the term "hero" has evolved with age. Reflect on the qualities or actions that define heroism for you at this stage in your life. If you were to choose a hero in your life now, who would it be and why?

TOMORROW: Contemplate the idea of being referred to as someone's hero in the future. Explore the emotions and thoughts that arise as you envision the possibility of playing such a significant and positive role in someone's life.

Ernest Hemingway, a literary giant whose influence on the 20th century was profound, once conveyed, 'Staying quiet doesn't mean I have nothing to say; it means I don't think you're read to hear my thoughts.' His wisdom suggests there is power in silence and questions others' readiness to engage with the depth of one's thoughts.

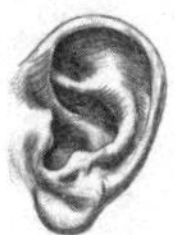

YESTERDAY: When you were younger were you more introverted or extroverted, and when you were unusually quiet, what did that mean?

TODAY: Reflect on your current life and consider how freely you share your thoughts with others. When is your silence more significant and when does it speak volumes? What factors influence your decision to speak or stay quiet, and how do you discern the right moment for each.

TOMORROW: Thinking about your future self how do you anticipate the way you speak to others will change? Will you share your wisdom through your words, or will your time be too precious to lend energy to meaningless conversations?

Rumi's introspective and insightful quote, "Yesterday I was clever, so I wanted to change the world. Today I am wise, so I am changing myself," emphasizes the fundamental importance of addressing our personal lives before taking on the challenges of the world. It underscores the wisdom of self-improvement as a prerequisite for positively influencing the broader external sphere.

YESTERDAY: Thinking about your past, what were your initial ideals regarding making a positive impact on the world? Reflect on any personal shortcomings that may have hindered your progress in striving towards your aspirations.

TODAY: As you've progressed through life and matured to your current stage, what personal growth and transformations have you undergone? How have these changes better equipped you to contribute to making the world a better place? Do you view yourself as a work in progress or do you feel you've reached a point where your impact will be significant?

TOMORROW: Envisioning the future, contemplate the aspects of personal growth you plan to continue working on. What will be your level of involvement in efforts to improve the world we live in? What continued goals and dreams will drive your commitment to both personal development and making a positive impact on the world?

Charlotte Brontë's quote, "Crying does not indicate that you are weak. Since birth, it has always been a sign that you are alive," suggests that there is strength in allowing oneself to release pent-up emotions. Individuals should embrace the courage to engage in what comes naturally, like crying, without the fear of judgment or ridicule.

YESTERDAY: Recall a moment from your past when you experienced a deep emotional release through crying. How did you feel, and did it initiate a healing process? Do you think you felt any hesitation or held back due to the fear of judgment from others?

TODAY: How has the way you processed your emotions, specifically crying evolved over the years? Have you learned anything recently about yourself and your emotions?

TOMORROW: Consider the trajectory of your emotional responses as you age. Do you anticipate crying more or less, and do you believe you'll become more apathetic or more empathetic? Reflect on the healthy emotional responses you currently exhibit and how you envision these influencing your future well-being.

Few lines from poetry evoke as many reflective moments as Robert Frost's from "The Road Not Taken": 'Two roads diverged in a wood, and I – I took the one less traveled by.' This poetic expression perfectly encapsulates the essence of our "what if" and "why not" moments, urging us to contemplate the choices that shape our journey.

YESTERDAY: : When reflecting on your past, what stands out as your most significant "what if" moment? Do you find yourself revisiting that particular time often, and if so, what thoughts consistently emerge during those reflections?

TODAY: What recent decisions have you made that you believe will have lasting impacts on your future? Are there any recent regrets that have been weighing on your mind?

TOMORROW: Fast forward to your future self, what regret do you hope to avoid when looking back on your past? Additionally, consider a "what if" scenario you hope to have explored, that would have played a role in your future.

The holiday classic, *A Christmas Story*, serves as a perfect example of how children ingeniously attempt to slip past the watchful eyes of their parents to fulfill their heart's desires, particularly when it comes to presents. The cautionary motherly advice that Ralphie's mom utters, 'You'll shoot your eye out,' still resonates in the ears of kids who find themselves grappling with a similar predicament.

YESTERDAY: Reflect on the words of wisdom your parents imparted to shield and protect you from danger while you were growing up. What guidance did they give you that helped you better understand the world around you?

TODAY: When contemplating the present world, what aspects concern or worry you the most? What dangers trouble you, increasing your unease about the state of the world we live in?

TOMORROW: Envisioning a future where you have children or grandchildren, consider the advice you would pass down to prepare and guide them for potential dangers. Reflect on the wisdom and insights you hope to impart to the next generation to help them navigate challenges and uncertainties in the world.

'Don't cross an ocean for someone who wouldn't cross a puddle for you.' This pearl of wisdom serves as a reminder to be discerning in the energy and efforts we invest in relationships."

YESTERDAY: Consider a relationship from your past where you invested significant time and emotional energy, only to find that the effort yielded little or no positive outcome. Reflect on the dynamics of that relationship, and the lessons you learned.

TODAY: Reflect on your current criteria when building relationships, whether they be friendships or otherwise. How have past relationships influenced and shaped your present approach.

TOMORROW: Envisioning your future, and the maturity that comes with age, do you anticipate placing more emphasis on preserving and protecting existing relationships, or will you be open to meeting new people and exploring new opportunities? How will your priorities and values evolve in regard to your social connections?

The phrase "Work hard, play hard" emphasizes the importance of achieving a harmonious balance between the demands of work and the pleasures of personal life. This philosophy suggests that dedicated effort and diligence in professional pursuits is complemented by an equally intentional commitment to leisure and personal well-being.

YESTERDAY: Reflecting on the past, how has your work ethic evolved? Did you prioritize more play or more work when you were younger, and how has this balance shifted over time?

TODAY: Share your current perspective on the concept of "work hard, play hard." Additionally, consider if there are specific challenges in your daily life that impact the application of this concept and how you are navigating those challenges.

TOMORROW: Looking ahead to retirement, consider whether you envision allocating more time for leisure activities or maintaining a work-focused outlook. Reflect on the factors influencing this decision and how your priorities may shift as you approach this significant life stage.

Mother Teresa offered sincere words of wisdom: "The good you do today will often be forgotten. Do good anyway." Her sentiment underscores the enduring value of doing good deeds without expecting recognition or acknowledgment.

YESTERDAY: Regarding your past, recall the earliest good deed you remember doing? What inspired you to take that action, and how did the experience make you feel?

TODAY: If you were to create a mission statement for yourself that embodies your philosophy on doing good deeds, what would it say? Consider whether this mission statement reflects any personal growth over time or if it has been a fundamental part of your values since youth.

TOMORROW: Looking ahead, do you have any specific plans or goals centered around doing good deeds or giving back in a deeper, more meaningful way? How much of your life will be dedicating to helping others?

Tom Bodett's insightful quote reflects on the contrasting approaches to learning: "In school, you're taught a lesson and then given a test. In life, you're given a test that teaches you a lesson." This perspective personifies the idea that our life experiences often serve as our most profound teachers.

YESTERDAY: Reflecting on your early life, consider the life lessons that were challenging for you to adjust to. Were there particular lessons that required repetition before you fully grasped them? How did they shape your personal growth and understanding?

TODAY: In your recent experiences, what valuable lesson or skill have you acquired that is currently proving beneficial? Has this newfound knowledge empowered you to share your insights and wisdom with someone else who may be facing a similar situation?

TOMORROW: Envisioning the next decade or more, what do you hope to have learned? Is there a particular life lesson you've been grappling with that you aim to conquer? If so, how will significantly help you as you navigate your future?

The question asked most frequently on college and job applications, as well as in focus group screening forms and general conversations, is: If you could have dinner with one person, living or dead, who would it be, and why?

YESTERDAY: In your younger years, if you could have had dinner with anyone, who would it have been, and what significance would that have held for you?

TODAY: Thinking about now, from a more mature perspective, who would you love to have dinner with and why?

TOMORROW: Looking ahead into the future, do you anticipate choosing the same person to have dinner with as you did today? What factors or changes in your life might influence your choice?

A remote control gives us the power to fast forward, rewind, and pause a movie or show, offering convenience and ensuring nothing is missed. Contemplate how different life would be if it came with a remote, allowing you to navigate through time and experiences with similar ease.

YESTERDAY: If life possessed a rewind button just like a TV remote, which chapter or part of your life would you choose to revisit and alter? Is there a specific moment or decision you would opt to change or handle differently?

TODAY: If you could metaphorically press pause on your life right now, how you would capitalize on that time? What would you do to make the most of the pause?

TOMORROW: What if you could press fast forward (just like a remote control) what part of your future life would you like to skip ahead to see and why? Do you think what you'd see will make an impact on how you life your life now?

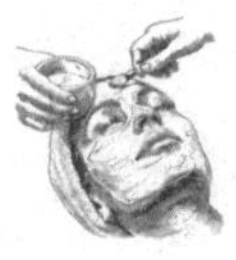

Self-care has emerged as a recent trend, gaining momentum alongside the growing awareness of mental health concerns. It involves the mindful practice of actively safeguarding one's well-being and happiness, especially during periods of stress.

YESTERDAY: Reflecting on your past, consider how well you prioritized taking care of your mind and body. Did you consistently make self-care a priority, or were there choices that you now recognize as less beneficial and impacting your well-being today? What decisions have shaped your mental and physical health over time?

TODAY: In the present, where mindfulness and prioritizing self-care and mental health are considered essential, how do you perceive this lifestyle? Do you find genuine value in adopting these practices as a way of life, or do you view it as a passing trend?

TOMORROW: Envisioning your future self, where health becomes a more significant concern with age, how do you anticipate your current prioritization of self-care evolving? Do you foresee a heightened focus on well-being, adjustments to your self-care practices, or any other changes to ensure optimal health as you navigate the aging process?

The word 'thrive' holds multiple inspiring meanings, both accurately encapsulating its powerful essence. To thrive is to grow vigorously, flourish, and progress toward or realize a goal, whether despite or because of life's circumstances.

YESTERDAY: Reflecting on your childhood, what specific factors contributed to you thriving or hindered your growth. Do you think these influences made a lasting impact on your character, mindset, and overall well-being?

TODAY: In the current moment, what aspects make you feel like you're thriving? How are you actively blooming and flourishing in your current circumstances? Reflect on the elements of your life that contribute to a sense of growth and fulfillment.

TOMORROW: Thinking about your future how important is it for you to continue thriving as opposed to just existing? What do you anticipate you'll need to attain this as you adjust to your body and mind's ever-changing needs?

The expression 'birds of a feather flock together' conveys that individuals with similar traits or interests tend to associate and engage in activities together. Additionally, it implies that one's character is reflected in the company they keep.

YESTERDAY: Reflecting on the "birds of a feather" phrase, consider the company you kept in the past. Do you believe the people you surrounded yourself with accurately reflected who you were at that time?

TODAY: Thinking about your current inner circle and friends, how has it evolved as you've matured? Have you retained some of your old friends, or have your needs in friendship shifted based on the direction your life has taken?

TOMORROW: : Envisioning your future, do you anticipate seeking new connections that align with your evolving outlook and needs, or do you believe your current relationships will withstand the test of time? Will your future path lead you to "flock" to others who share similar interests, forming new bonds or will you invest in strengthening existing ones?

"Control, Alt, Delete" is a keyboard combination enabling users to view and terminate running programs simultaneously. This functionality has inspired a self-help mantra: "Ctrl - Control your thoughts, Alt - Alter your Attitude, Del - Delete Negativity." This translates the keyboard command into a practical guide for managing one's mindset and emotions.

YESTERDAY: Reflecting on your past and the journey of self-discovery, how did you navigate negativity, control your thoughts, and adjust your attitude when needed? Did this involve parental discipline, or were you proactive in taking independent steps to shape your mindset and outlook?

TODAY: Focusing on your present life, do you wrestle with negativity or have trouble controlling your thoughts or emotions? How do you handle these issues when they arise, and what have you learned about yourself through the years that helps you make adjustments?

TOMORROW: Anticipating your future, what current practices are you incorporating to facilitate self-improvement down the road? Is there a specific aspect of your mindset you find challenging and hope to gain better control over as you progress? Reflect on the strategies you're implementing now to pave the way for personal growth and positive changes in the future.

While the phrase 'timing is everything' has numerous adaptations and interpretations across various contexts, its meaning remains the same. Sometimes in life it's all about the timing.

YESTERDAY: Looking at life in the rearview mirror, have you ever found yourself in a situation where perfect timing played a significant role, or conversely, where being in the wrong place at the wrong time had memorable consequences?

TODAY: In your current life stage, what insights have you gained about the importance of timing? Have your instincts sharpened to the point where you can gauge when it's the right time for certain actions or decisions?

TOMORROW: Envisioning tomorrow, what are you hopeful about getting the timing just right for? Consider the dream or vision you have and reflect on the elements that need to align to make it a reality.

Winston Churchill's quote, 'Never give up on something that you can't go a day without thinking about,' serves as a poignant reminder of the significance of pursuing the things we hold dear.

YESTERDAY: When you were younger, what held importance to you during that time? What activities, hobbies, sports, or games occupied your mind and thoughts, and why did these pursuits matter to you?

TODAY: Is there a particular area of interest, desire, or dream that has been forefront in your mind lately? How are you pursuing it?

TOMORROW: Visualizing your future, what do you see yourself never going a day without? What occupies your thoughts so intensely you could never give up on it?

Oscar Wilde beautifully expressed the profound impact of small joys on our lives when he remarked, 'Simple pleasures are the last healthy refuge in a complex world.' This sentiment encapsulates the enduring value of finding happiness in the little things.

YESTERDAY: Reflecting on your youth, what were the simple pleasures that brought you joy? Consider the uncomplicated delights and activities that held a special place in your heart during that time.

TODAY: Looking at your life presently, what little things would you miss if you didn't have them? Have you developed a deeper appreciation for life's simple pleasures compared to when you were younger? How has your perspective on these aspects of life evolved over time?

TOMORROW: As you continue to grow and transform through the stages of life, what little things and simple pleasures are you looking forward to the most? What small joys do you think you will add to your list as you get older that aren't that significant now?

The Hawaiian way of life is deeply guided by the aloha spirit, a tradition sacred to the islanders. Within their 'rules to live by' philosophy, a rule that stands out states: "The best things in life aren't things." This thoughtful advice personifies prioritizing experiences and relationships over material possessions to have a more meaningful life.

YESTERDAY: Think back on your younger years, were you more inclined towards materialism, or were you taught to value meaningful experiences? What influenced and shaped your perspective on possessions versus experiences during that period of your life?

TODAY: As an outsider looking in, does your life reflect a person who prioritizes and enjoys more meaningful pursuits or does your surroundings reflect a heavy emphasis on material possessions?

TOMORROW: What significant and purposeful experiences do you hope to have in the future and what are you willing to sacrifice to ensure they happen?

Henry David Thoreau's priceless advice says: 'Go confidently in the direction of your dreams. Live the life you have imagined.' These words serve as a beacon, encouraging individuals to pursue their aspirations with confidence and manifest the life they envision.

YESTERDAY: What inspired or influenced this vision, and did it ever resemble a fairy tale in your imagination? Describe the elements of the earliest aspirations that shaped your dreams for the future.

TODAY: Thinking about Thoreau's quote in the present sense, 'Go confidently in the direction of your dreams. Live the life you have imagined," what steps are you taking to manifest the life of your dreams? Describe what your dream looks like.

TOMORROW: As you reach the end of your life and cast a retrospective gaze back, what you hope to see? What do you want most for your life that you've not fulfilled yet?

Maya Angelou's poignant words from *I Know Why The Caged Bird Sings* depict the caged bird's yearning for freedom. The bird's song, with a mix of fear and longing, resonates even on a distant hill, symbolizing the universal desire for liberation despite facing the unknown challenges ahead.

YESTERDAY: Reflecting on past phases of your life, was there a moment when you felt caged or imprisoned by certain thoughts or an experience? What circumstances led to that feeling of constraint? How did you navigate or overcome such challenges?

TODAY: Presently what gives you a sense of freedom and allows you to explore endless horizons and seize opportunities, fostering a sense of liberation and unrestricted potential?

TOMORROW: Anticipating years into your future, do you have concerns that certain circumstances might induce feelings of helplessness or impede your ability to feel free? How can you proactively approach these challenges to preserve a sense of freedom and empowerment in the face of life's uncertainties?

A pencil consists of two essential parts: the lead and the eraser. The eraser plays a crucial role in the writing instrument, enabling users to correct mistakes. Bearing this in mind, if life had an eraser, what possibilities for correction and improvement might unfold?

YESTERDAY: Are elements from your past that you would consider erasing in order to enhance your path toward accomplishing your dreams, what specific facets would you target? How do you believe correcting or changing these aspects would positively impact your future?

TODAY: From a present standpoint, if you could erase something out of your life right now that is affecting your happiness or ability to achieve your goals, what would it be?

TOMORROW: Considering your family's future, what aspects or concerns would you like to eradicate or ease to alleviate worries permanently? How do you believe eliminating these challenges would contribute to a brighter and more secure future for your family?

Lao Tzu's wisdom was evident with this quote, "New beginnings are often disguised as painful endings," It's synonymous with the old adage you have to endure a little rain to witness a rainbow.

YESTERDAY: Recall a moment from your past where something meaningful to you ended, and the pain seemed it would last forever. What helped you get through the experience?

TODAY: Consider a painful experience from your past that eventually blossomed into a beautiful new beginning, contributing to your present life.

TOMORROW: Contemplate the intersection of your past and present when faced with the conclusion of a specific relationship, career, or experience of loss. Reflect on how it changed you and identify the positive aspects that have emerged. How will these experiences make your future richer and more fulfilling?

The idiomatic expression "in the hot seat" refers to an individual who has landed in trouble or has come under scrutiny for something negative.

YESTERDAY: When you were younger describe a time when you found yourself in the hot seat. What led to you getting into trouble and what did you learn from the experience?

TODAY: Reflecting on your past experiences when you faced trouble, what specific incident taught you the most valuable lesson? How does this lesson influence your present actions, prompting you to think twice before acting and ensuring you stay out of the hot seat now?

TOMORROW: Thinking ahead to future situations if a friend, your child or another family member finds themselves in trouble, what valuable advice will you share with them?

Everybody loves a fairytale as evident by the popularity of *Cinderella, The Little Mermaid* and *Beauty and the Beast*. In recent years the mantra "fight for your fairytale" was coined inspiring a reality where fairytales are possible, if you just believe.

YESTERDAY: During your childhood, which fairytale or fairytale character resonated with you the most, and why? Explore how this identification influenced your earliest vision for your life and the impact it had on shaping your aspirations and perceptions during that formative period.

TODAY: Thinking about your life now, how does it compare with the vision or fairytale you dreamed about during your younger years? Has surpassed your expectations, fallen short, or taken a different path? What elements that have contributed to this alignment or deviation and reflect on how your perceptions and aspirations may have evolved over time.

TOMORROW: Envisioning the future of your life, describe the fairytale vision you would love to see unfold. Paint a picture of the ideal scenario, including elements of success, fulfillment, and happiness. Share the aspects of this vision that hold significance for you and contribute to your sense of a fairy tale ending.

Imagine if iconic artists such as Picasso, Monet, and Da Vinci had entrusted their paintbrushes to someone else; the world would be deprived of the breathtaking masterpieces we cherish today. That's why the saying: 'You are the artist of your own life; don't hand the paintbrush to anyone else,' is so important because it urges individuals to take control of their life and actively craft a unique masterpiece all their own.

YESTERDAY: Reflecting on the earlier years of your life, consider your journey as a painting. Describe the colors, strokes, and themes that represent the various phases, experiences, and transitions you've encountered. Explore how the canvas of your life has evolved, capturing the unique tapestry that forms the artwork of your personal journey.

TODAY: In the present tense of your life, identify the aspects or areas that you are fiercely protective over, ones you would never allow anyone else to hold the paintbrush for. Explore the boundaries you've established and the elements of your life that you consider deeply personal and off-limits to external influence.

TOMORROW: Visualize your future as a painting, describe the elements that compose this artwork and what they represent. Use your words like brush strokes to symbolize your aspirations, dreams, and desired experiences. Explain the significance of each element and what you hope your future will look like through the visual representation of your artistic vision.

The song "Don't Worry Be Happy," by Bobby McFerrin was an instant hit. People soon adopted the tune's carefree tone as their daily motto, and even though it was released in the 80s it's still relevant today.

YESTERDAY: Recall a moment from your past where you were carefree. What signs were present that signaled your happiness during that time? Reflect on the elements, emotions, or activities that contributed to the sense of carefree joy in that moment.

TODAY: Share the motto you have adopted in your present-day life and how it contributes to prioritizing your happiness? Additionally, are there specific worries or concerns that tend to interfere with your ability to experience joy and contentment?

TOMORROW: Looking ahead to your future, consider actions you can take now to foster a "don't worry, be happy" outlook. Reflect on potential strategies, habits, or mindset shifts that can contribute to a more positive and joyful perspective.

"Health is wealth" serves as a contemporary rendition of the age-old saying, "An apple a day keeps the doctor away." Both expressions convey a lighthearted perspective, playfully emphasizing the crucial role of maintaining good health in our overall well-being.

YESTERDAY: In your younger years, did you prioritize your health, and if so, what motivated or influenced that choice? Alternatively, if health wasn't a primary focus, what factors contributed to that perspective?

TODAY: Reflecting on your present-day health, identify any concerns you may have, and elaborate on the measures you are currently taking to ensure a healthy and enduring life. Consider lifestyle choices, habits, or preventive actions that contribute to your overall well-being.

TOMORROW: Do you harbor concerns about your future health, whether due to hereditary conditions or poor choices made in the past? How are you working through these concerns now, to create a smoother path forward?

Chicken soup, known for its comforting warmth, serves as both a remedy for illness and a nostalgic connection to home. Beyond its culinary significance, the concept inspired "Chicken Soup for the Soul," a collection of short stories exploring themes of kindness, love, compassion, and support, showcasing the positive aspects of human nature.

YESTERDAY: Reflecting on your childhood, was there something specific that brought you comfort, warmth, or made you feel safe? Explore the memories associated with this comforting element and consider its significance in shaping your early sense of security.

TODAY: Thinking about your life now, what do you equate with a warm bowl of chicken soup? What comforts you when you feel homesick, ill or just need to feel loved?

TOMORROW: As you contemplate the future, do you foresee the need for more comfort as you navigate life's changes, or do you envision taking on the role of a comforter to help those around you feel secure? Reflect on what you would provide to others that brought you comfort, offering a sense of well-being and support.

This deep quote by C.S. Lewis, "The fact that our heart yearns for something earth can't supply, is proof that heaven must be our home," suggests that the inherent longing in our hearts indicates a need for a connection to something greater beyond earthly experiences.

YESTERDAY: Recall the earliest moments when you thought about spiritual concepts like God, heaven, and faith? Were there individuals who influenced your perspective on faith or religion during your formative years?

TODAY: Thinking about your life right now, describe your current outlook on faith and religion. How has it evolved from your past to the present and what factors have strengthened or introduced doubts in your journey? Additionally, share the role your spiritual life plays in your day-to-day experiences.

TOMORROW: As you grow older do you think your spiritual life will grow or remain the same and what factors may contribute to a change on your outlook or perspective when it comes to your faith?

The expression "turning a blind eye" implies the act of deliberately ignoring or overlooking something, often with the awareness that it could have negative consequences.

YESTERDAY: Recall a past experience or time when you turned a blind eye to something you shouldn't have, and it ended up impacting your life in a negative way.

TODAY: Reflecting on past mistakes of ignoring things you shouldn't have; share the lessons you've learned. How do you currently address negative situations in your present-day life to avoid repeating troublesome experiences. What strategies have you've adopted to navigate challenges more effectively.

TOMORROW: As you navigate your future, how you've become more attentive and mindful to prevent negative impacts on yourself and your family. What proactive measures are you considering ensuring a more positive and informed path forward?

"The Tortoise and the Hare" imparts two valuable lessons. The first highlights the perils of boasting about one's abilities, as seen when the rabbit mocks the tortoise for being slow. The second is the power of self-belief and persistence, emphasizing that significant accomplishments can be achieved when we have confidence in ourselves and refuse to give up.

YESTERDAY: When you think about the fable "tortoise and the hare" and apply it to your younger years, which animal do you identify with most? What aspects of them remind you of your years growing up and why?

TODAY: In the race of your present-day life, relating it to the tale of the Tortoise and the Hare, what humbling moments have you had and what did they teach you? What are you learning about yourself through this process?

TOMORROW: Looking ahead to your future, what kind of pace do you want to establish for your life and what benefits will that provide to enhance your journey? Thinking about how far you've come already, how can you strengthen confidence in yourself to stay the course?

Tom Phelan's memoir, *We Were Rich and We Didn't Know It*, serves as a tribute to his upbringing in 1940s Ireland. Set in a time before rural electrification, telephones, and indoor plumbing, the narrative reflects an era where bicycles were the primary mode of travel. Despite the lack of material wealth, the memoir underscores the richness found in the love of family and the priceless memories created during that period.

YESTERDAY: Reflecting on your younger years, did you ever feel a sense of lack because your friends or neighbors had things you didn't? Looking back, do you still have those feelings or have your perspectives evolved over time?

TODAY: Focusing on your current life, how are you rich in the non-material sense? What things do you have in your life that are priceless?

TOMORROW: Thinking about your tomorrow, the future you will have what values and traditions do you want to embrace that give your life depth and meaning? How will you impart these to future generations in your family?

The old aphorism "fool me once, shame on you; fool me twice, shame on me" serves as a warning that after being tricked once, one should learn from one's mistakes and take precautions to avoid being deceived in the same way again.

YESTERDAY: Recall a moment from your past where someone tricked you. How did you feel, and how did you handle the situation? Did this experience bring about any changes in you, and what impact did it have on your relationship with this person?

TODAY: Reflecting on your present life, do you believe you would still fall for the same schemes you experienced in the past? How does being deceived by someone impact your trust in others?

TOMORROW: Thinking about all the times you dealt with foolishness and deception, do you think you would trick or scheme someone in the future? Why or why not?

Despite being a fictional character from the television series *Sons of Anarchy*, Piney Winston's words carry profound weight: "We all do damage. Character is determined by how we repair it."

YESTERDAY: Consider a past relationship, be it with a friend or family member, where damage was done. Have you managed to repair that bond, or are there still unresolved issues? Does the state of this relationship speak to your character, their character, or a combination of both?

TODAY: In your present life, how quickly do you forgive when you have issues with someone? Do you give them a chance to make amends, or do you tend to shut people out as a means of self-preservation? Reflect on how you handle conflict and consider the impact unresolved conflicts have on you.

TOMORROW: Contemplating your future relationships, what insights have you gained regarding forgiveness, reconciliation, and your approach to managing interpersonal challenges? Consider the differences you envision in how you'll handle conflict compared to the past. Share your thoughts on the growth and changes you anticipate in your future approach to relationships and resolving conflicts.

Self-help books have been instrumental in assisting individuals with a range of issues, with a predominant emphasis on bolstering confidence. A recurring theme underscores the importance of achieving a healthy self-esteem by finding a balance between confidence and humility.

YESTERDAY: Have you ever sought help from a self-help book in the past? If so, why did you choose this form of guidance, and did it help? If not, what reservations, if any, do you have about seeking help from self-help books? Do you believe there are other resources that are more effective for you?

TODAY: Describe your present-day self-esteem and how it has changed from your past. Have you found a balance between confidence and humility? What are you currently working on in that specific area?

TOMORROW: Envisioning your future self, what aspects of growth would you like to see in terms of self-esteem, confidence, and humility? Describe the best version of yourself and the qualities that will contribute to a well-balanced and positive self-perception.

Steve Maraboli is a transformative speaker, bestselling author, and Behavioral Scientist. He brings his influential voice to various topics, and one of his most impactful statements is, "If the feelings are mutual, the effort will be equal."

YESTERDAY: Reflecting on your past, have you ever felt that you invested more effort into a relationship, employment, or team without receiving an equal level of energy or enthusiasm in return? Conversely, have you been in a position where you may not have reciprocated the same level of engagement? Describe how you felt and what happened.

TODAY: Presently if you encountered a similar situation what signs signal that a breakdown in the flow of the partnership is eminent? What have you learned from past experiences that will help you maintain balanced and mutually beneficial connections.

TOMORROW: Thinking about the future, what are the things you will no longer tolerate in partnerships or relationships? Describe your vision of a mutual effort in both your personal life and work ethic. Share the standards and expectations you aspire to uphold in your future connections to ensure a balanced and fulfilling partnership.

"Coloring outside the lines" is an idiom that encourages breaking free from conventional rules and thinking creatively. Similarly, the metaphor "thinking outside the box" emphasizes the importance of approaching situations with unconventional and innovative perspectives. These expressions inspire a departure from traditional norms and encourage creative thinking.

YESTERDAY: Reflect on your younger years and recall the first time you became aware of your creative abilities. Describe a specific instance where you colored outside the lines and how that sense of creative freedom fueled your imagination and self-expression.

TODAY: In your present day, when faced with challenges or obstacles, how do you tap into creative thinking? Does thinking outside the box come naturally to you, or do you find it necessary to dig deep? Explore how your creativity influences your ability to approach problems unconventionally and share insights into your process of innovative thinking.

TOMORROW: Apply the terms "coloring outside the lines" and "think outside the box" to your future, what do you see? How does this tie into future endeavors, adventures and relationships?

Dr. Seuss imparts valuable life lessons through his whimsical words, with the quote, "Today you are You, that is truer than true. There is no one alive who is Youer than You." This lesson emphasizes the importance of authenticity and the uniqueness inherent in each individual.

YESTERDAY: When you were younger how did friends and family describe you, and how did that differ from how you saw yourself? What unique personality traits did you develop at a young age?

TODAY: Viewing yourself today as a quilt, where bits of fabric represent the elements that make up your identity, explore the fabric of your DNA. Reflect on what makes you uniquely you and how you have embraced and woven together different aspects of your individuality into a cohesive and beautiful expression of self.

TOMORROW: Reflecting on your present self, are there any quirks or aspects of your personality that you are hesitant to carry into your future, or have you resolved to accept and embrace every facet of yourself?

The expression "apple of my eye" is a term of endearment used to convey deep affection and fondness for someone special. Meaning this person holds a special place in your heart.

YESTERDAY: Recall a time from your past when someone doted on you the most. Identify the person who unquestionably considered you the apple of their eye, and reflect on what their affection meant to you during that time.

TODAY: Reflect on the person in your present life who is the apple of your eye. Describe the emotions they evoke in you and explore how your personal growth has been influenced through your love for them.

TOMORROW: In envisioning the future, consider what else, aside from people, could be the apple of your eye. Explore how this broader perspective might enhance your life in new and meaningful ways.

The law of attraction predicates that one's thoughts and feelings shape their life. Proponents of this law argue that the energy an individual emits into the world determines what they attract back into their life.

YESTERDAY: Reflecting on past encounters and experiences, analyze the kind of energy you were emitting and attracting. Consider how this aligns with the principles of the law of attraction theory.

TODAY: What is your present take on the law of attraction? Reflecting on this concept, do you find yourself adjusting your mindset and actions to align more with positive thinking, fostering an environment conducive to attracting favorable outcomes and experiences? Do you have a different opinion on why good or bad things happen in life?

TOMORROW: As you look to your future do you anticipate embracing positivity in your thoughts and actions to shape a more favorable reality that invites fulfillment and success? What are you hoping to attract more of in your life and what steps are you taking to ensure that happens?

"And then I realized the fire was always burning within me, but the flames were busy keeping everyone else warm." These profound words from Morgan Richard Olivier evoke a powerful pause, urging introspection.

YESTERDAY: Reflecting on your past, consider the personal sacrifices you've made to prioritize others over yourself. Which areas of your life were most affected by these choices, and how did this impact you emotionally?

TODAY: Thinking about where you are in your life right now, do you have a fire burning within? Are you making the most of that fire, or are you exhausting the flames spreading yourself too thin for others and not making time for your own passions?

TOMORROW: In the future, if you find the spark within you has dimmed, how will you get it back? Think about actions you can take today to preserve that spark, creating a reservoir of inspiration to reignite your fire when needed.

When purchasing a product, particularly electronics, it often includes a user manual. This guide instructs users on how to operate the product, care for it, and troubleshoot any issues. Imagine if life were similarly accompanied by such a comprehensive set of instructions.

YESTERDAY: Consider a past time when a "user manual" could have been beneficial. Identify a situation or period in your life where clear instructions would have guided you. Reflect on whether having such guidance might have influenced the outcome.

TODAY: If you could blink and make a user manual appear for something you're struggling with right now, what would it be and what specific help are you looking for?

TOMORROW: Thinking about your journey up to this point, if you were to draft a user manual based on your life experiences, what situation or life phase would you address, and how do you anticipate your insights could guide and assist others in the future?

When viewing a movie at home or elsewhere, you may encounter a warning that appears, stating: 'This film has been modified from its original version.' This disclaimer serves as an acknowledgment that the content has undergone alterations and is not presented in its original form.

YESTERDAY: Looking back how would you describe your growing pains? Was it a mix of self-discovery, adapting to new responsibilities, and facing uncertainties? Did you feel like yourself amidst the transformation, or were parts of you unrecognizable?

TODAY: Looking at yourself in the mirror today, how have you been modified from the original version, and do you like the current version of yourself better or less than the original?

TOMORROW: Looking ahead as you continue to have various life experiences, what transformations do you anticipate occurring naturally as you mature, and what fundamental aspects of your authentic self would you like to preserve?

Siskel and Ebert, a popular American film critic duo, were renowned for their witty banter and succinct movie reviews, often surmised by their iconic thumbs up or thumbs down reactions. Their opinions were widely regarded as gospel in assessing the quality of motion pictures.

YESTERDAY: Think about your past as a movie, now write a review from the perspective of a movie critic. What were the highlights and what can viewers expect from the sequel?

TODAY: Your present day is the sequel to part one of the movie. Describe how the characters have changed and what's going on in their lives now. Remember, to write this from a movie critics point of view.

TOMORROW: Thinking about your future, and your life as a trilogy, write what you want the coming attractions to look like in the next movie of this franchise which is your life.

The phrase "hitting rock bottom" suggests reaching a point where one feels they have nowhere else to go but up. Many view these moments as opportunities for significant personal growth. It becomes crucial for individuals to understand the factors that led to that low point, and utilize the experience to avoid similar situations in the future while fostering self-improvement.

YESTERDAY: Recall a time from your past where you hit rock bottom. How did you get there, and did you recover? Describe your journey and the process.

TODAY: If you reached a low point now, what did your past troubles teach you that can help you get back on track today? Have you built a dependable support system that you can reach out to in tough times?

TOMORROW: If you have a friend or loved one that hits rock bottom in the future, what words of wisdom can you share? What did your struggles teach you that you feel would benefit someone else in a similar situation?

The Golden Girls are a pop culture obsession, so much so they are considered a national treasure in some countries. Each Golden Girl is beloved for her distinctive personality and endearing quirks. Each one brings something unique to the table and that's what makes their friendship and bond so magnetic.

YESTERDAY: Reflecting on your life growing up, what personality traits did you possess that were people drawn to? How do you think you made them feel?

TODAY: Thinking about your life currently, what personality traits are you drawn to in others, what feels magnetic to you? How do those specific traits in others compliment yours?

TOMORROW: Looking ahead to your golden years, which Golden Girl reminds you of yourself? What about them resonate with you and do you think these traits will help you navigate the later chapter of your life?

The age-old saying "count your blessings" continues to hold relevance, emphasizing the importance of gratitude as a key component in a happy life. The timeless nature of this sentiment is reflected in the contemporary trend of gratitude journals, where individuals consciously document and reflect on the positive aspects of their lives.

YESTERDAY: Reflecting on the past several years, what are the things you are grateful for, and have you cultivated a habit of counting your blessings?

TODAY: In your present-day life do you use a gratitude journal, why or why not and do you think focusing on gratitude will improve your mood, outlook and overall happiness?

TOMORROW: Anticipating the days to come, what do you hope to have in your life, and do you believe appreciating your life as it is now will sow the seeds for a hopeful future?

When someone tells you 'a penny for your thoughts,' they are expressing curiosity about what is occupying your mind, especially when you appear deeply engrossed in thought and perhaps reserved or quiet.

YESTERDAY: Looking back to your younger years what used to occupy your thoughts, what was always on your mind? How did the subject of your thoughts change over time?

TODAY: Reflecting on your present day, do you find yourself preoccupied with numerous thoughts, occasionally getting lost in contemplation? Are you an over thinker and if so, what helps you to work through your thoughts?

TOMORROW: Anticipating your future, how do you foresee your thoughts and thought processes evolving as you mature? Do you believe you can overcome any negative thinking patterns you may have developed?

The motivational affirmation "no risk, no reward" encapsulates the idea that embracing risks is integral to achieving significant rewards. The philosophy behind this phrase, explores how taking calculated risks can lead to valuable lessons and personal growth.

YESTERDAY: Recall a time where you just took a risk and went for it. Did it pay off, and if so, what was the reward and how did it change your life? If it wasn't quite successful, did you learn anything from it, and are you glad you took a chance?

TODAY: If you were going to take a chance on something right now, in this very moment, what would it be? Describe your desired outcome and how it could alter your future? What if anything is holding you back from taking this leap?

TOMORROW: Contemplating your future, do you think you will ever get to a point in your life where taking a risk is too risky and no reward could justify taking a chance? Or do you think taking risks is what keeps life interesting?

The poet and scholar Rumi once stated, "If you are irritated by every rub, how will you be polished?" It explores the idea that facing and overcoming irritations and constructive criticism contributes to personal growth and refinement, much like the process of polishing.

YESTERDAY: Reflecting on your past, how did you react when your parents or teachers offered guidance and correction? Did your attitude towards discipline influence your journey forward, and if yes, how?

TODAY: How do you respond to constructive criticism presently? Are you open to receiving feedback or is this area of your life still a work in progress? How open are you to giving feedback to others?

TOMORROW: Thinking of yourself in terms of a rock, what areas of your life would you like to see more polished in the future? What future goals do you have that makes this transformation necessary?

The quest for purpose and the pursuit of passion have intrigued philosophers throughout history. It seems to be the question of our lifetime. Today, this existential theme persists, and is echoed in Billie Eilish's song, "What Was I Made For?

YESTERDAY: Reflecting on your past, how old were you when you pondered or questioned your life's purpose? Have you actively taken any steps to explore and understand the underlying reasons for your existence?

TODAY: Thinking about your life present day, have you made any progress determining how you fit into this big wide world?

TOMORROW: Looking ten years ahead into the future and pondering Billie's song, if someone were to ask, "What were you made for?" how would you respond? Additionally, what steps are you currently taking to fulfill your perceived life's purpose?

The phrase "Money doesn't grow on trees" is a common diatribe from parents, reminding their children that money is earned through hard work and should be spent judiciously.

YESTERDAY: In your younger years, did your parents ever convey the saying "money doesn't grow on trees"? Were you taught about money as you grew up, and if so, how has that influenced your current perspective and approach to handling finances?

TODAY: In contemplating your present life, how would you describe your relationship with money? What recent insights have you gained about how money works, and what are your current financial goals?

TOMORROW: Looking ahead several years down the road, what is your ideal financial outlook? What role will money play in your future and what are you doing now to make your future more secure?

Prentis Hemphill eloquently expressed, "Boundaries are the distance at which I can love you and me simultaneously." This sentiment reinforces the idea that boundaries aren't intended to alienate but rather to establish a healthy balance between individuals.

YESTERDAY: Reflecting on your past, was there a moment when you didn't establish boundaries and felt taken advantage of or experienced someone crossing a line? What valuable lessons did you learn from that particular experience?

TODAY: Thinking about the present, what boundaries do you have established and how do they serve you in your relationships today? Is there something specific you're protecting?

TOMORROW: Thinking about your future, what additional boundaries do you anticipate having to set? What have you learned thus far about establishing boundaries that will help you later in life?

An influencer is an individual who leverages their platform to endorse and promote curated products, aiming to influence a wide audience to make purchases. This has rapidly evolved into a lucrative career path in the era of digital marketing and social media.

YESTERDAY: Share a past experience with an influencer and describe your reaction. Were they effective, and what aspects of their platform did you appreciate or dislike?

TODAY: Would you considered becoming an influencer presently? How do you envision yourself in this role, and is it something you could find enjoyable? If you were to pursue this path, what niche would you focus on, and what aspects of your personality or content do you think others would resonate with and respond to?

TOMORROW: Contemplating an influencer career, do you believe it could evolve into a larger, more lucrative profession in the future? Is it viewed as a momentary source of income for fun, or do you anticipate it becoming the ideal entrepreneurial wave of the future?

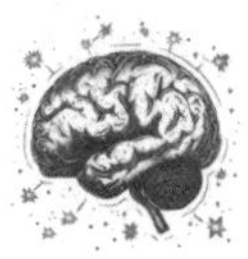

IQ stands for Intelligence Quotient. IQ tests are tools used to measure intellectual abilities and potential. They are designed to assess a broad range of cognitive skills, including reasoning, logic, and problem-solving. IQ is considered a measure of innate intelligence, something largely inherent from birth.

YESTERDAY: Did you ever take an IQ test while growing up? How significant was the importance of being perceived as smart for you, and how much emphasis did you place on intellect compared to appearance or beauty?

TODAY: In your present day, do you believe IQ tests still hold merit and value, or do you see them as an antiquated concept? What, in your opinion, constitutes the true test of intelligence? Describe how you view your personal intellect.

TOMORROW: Considering the future in the ever-expanding age of technology, how do you foresee intelligence and a person's potential being measured? How do you think the criteria for measuring abilities will evolve over time?

A philanthropist is an individual who contributes time, money, experience, skills, or talent to help create a better world. Philanthropy is open to anyone, regardless of status or net worth.

YESTERDAY: Recall a time from your past where you performed a charitable act. What did you do, how did it make you feel, and did it inspire you to do more good work?

TODAY: Thinking about your life now what causes or charities are important to you. Do you make an effort to get involved and get others involved. What specific aspects of these organizations and causes speak to you, why are they important?

TOMORROW: Contemplating your future, if you were to come into a significant windfall of money, how much would you allocate to causes you find worthy? Additionally, what type of philanthropist do you envision yourself becoming?

Recess serves as a vital part of the school day where students have the opportunity to engage in physical activities and social interactions with their peers. This break from academic studies allows them to recharge, both mentally and physically, promoting overall well-being.

YESTERDAY: Glancing back at your childhood years as you were growing up, how did you feel about recess? What did you like or dislike about it and how do you think it benefited you?

TODAY: In the present day, do you believe companies should incorporate recess for adults? Would taking breaks to play and unwind while still getting paid contribute to a healthier and more productive workspace? And, personally, would you enjoy having recess as part of your workday?

TOMORROW: Looking ahead to your future if you have kids or grandkids would you want them to have access to recess? How would you encourage them to play and take advantage of this time? Would you have any reservations about this playtime?

L'Oreal Paris is one of the leading brands in beauty. Their slogan "because you're worth it" not only lets their customers know they value them, but also serves as encouragement for individuals to recognize and appreciate their own worth.

YESTERDAY: Reflecting on your earlier years, did you believe you were worth it? How did you perceive and respect yourself in your youth, and how has that early relationship with yourself influenced the person you've become today? Was there an incident that altered your reflection of worthiness within yourself?

TODAY: In the present, how would you describe your relationship with yourself? What changes in recent years have influenced the way you view yourself? Have you worked through past issues in this area, so you have a healthier outlook on your worth?

TOMORROW: Looking ahead to the years to come, using the slogan "because you're worth it," consider and list all the things you believe you are worthy of. What aspects are currently missing from your life that you acknowledge as deserving and anticipate having in the future?

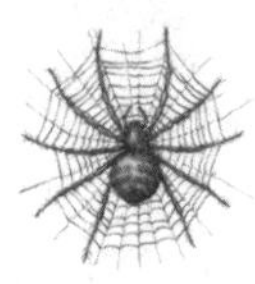

Although *Charlotte's Web* is a classic children's novel, its themes of relationships, life lessons, and morals transcend age and time, making it an enduring source of appreciation for readers of all ages.

YESTERDAY: Looking back was there a children's story, book or novel that helped you as you were growing up? Were there any character's you identified with or learned from that made your journey through adolescence easier?

TODAY: Consider something you're currently reading that is impacting your life. How is it adding value to your relationships and shaping your day-to-day outlook? Additionally, what's one of the most important things you've learned from a book that continues to assist you today?

TOMORROW: If you were to write a children's book in the future, what would be the central theme? Would it focus on lessons, morals, or provide entertainment? Considering the knowledge you've accumulated over the years, what elements could contribute to a compelling and valuable story for children?

Poetry, a distinct form of literature, serves as a means to express thoughts and feelings through the aesthetic qualities of language. The primary goal of teaching poetry lies in fostering enjoyment and appreciation. Poetic words and phrases inherently provide learners with a source of profound pleasure, nurturing genuine feelings and a true sense of enjoyment.

YESTERDAY: Reflecting on the past, when were you first introduced to poetry? Did you instantly develop an affinity for it, or did it take time to understand? Is there a specific poem or poet that stands out in your memory as the one who made you truly appreciate the beauty of poetry?

TODAY: If you had to choose a poem that mirrors you and your current life, what would it be, and why does this particular poem resonate with you? Additionally, how has your opinion or appreciation of poetry evolved over the years?

TOMORROW: Looking ahead, write a poem that reflects what you hope your future looks like. Be specific and descriptive, and even if you're not comfortable writing poems, give it your best shot. This is for your inspiration and a way to manifest your vision.

Moths are often attracted to the light of flames, a tendency that can lead to their demise. Therefore, when someone says you're acting like a moth to a flame, they may be suggesting that you are drawn to something potentially harmful, despite the known consequences.

YESTERDAY: Recall a moment when you were drawn to someone or something like a moth to a flame. Describe the emotions you felt and what transpired with your attraction. Was this experience a positive or negative moment for you?

TODAY: Thinking about this moment, if you were a moth, what would be the flame? Why or what about the flame is tempting and drawing you in? What are your expectations should you draw closer to the flame and what are the potential consequences?

TOMORROW: Contemplating your future, what is something from your past, already in your rearview mirror, that you were attracted to but proved to be detrimental? If this potential "flame" reappears, what steps can you take to prevent yourself from being drawn to it again like a moth?

The song "Flowers" by Miley Cyrus is a powerful anthem advocating self-empowerment and independence in the midst of life's challenges. It boldly defies the societal stigma that suggests individuals need external validation, whether from others or certain positions, to define their worth.

YESTERDAY: Reflecting on a past moment from your life, can you describe a specific time when a reminder, like the song "Flowers," could have inspired strength from within during moments of self-doubt or when you found yourself in a dark place?

TODAY: When you face challenges in your present life, how do you tap into your internal strength, and what gives you sense of empowerment? What aspects of current society make it difficult to maintain a sense of independence?

TOMORROW: Envisioning a brighter future, write about ways you can build on your confidence, self-empowerment and specific things you can do for yourself when faced with external pressures or challenges that may attempt to undermine your worth.

The term 'skeletons in the closet' is a colloquial expression used to describe secrets about someone that, if revealed, could damage their reputation or alter how others perceive them.

YESTERDAY: Reflect on a moment from your past when you discovered a secret not meant to be shared or heard a rumor that could harm someone's character. How did you navigate gossip and rumors about others, and how has your approach evolved as you've matured?

TODAY: In your current life, how trustworthy do you consider yourself in keeping other people's secrets, and is there anyone you would entrust with your own? Additionally, how do you generally feel about the concept of secrets?

TOMORROW: Do you have any skeletons in your closet currently, that if got out could potentially be detrimental to your future? What steps can you take now to neutralize the power those secrets have so they can't be used against you later?

Bedtime stories were opportunities for parents to bond with their child and played a crucial role in their development. The shared experience not only created precious moments but also provided insights into a child's perspective as they engaged with the plot, characters, and setting of the book.

YESTERDAY: Reflecting on your earlier years, what role did bedtime stories play in your life? Were they read to you by someone, and do you have a favorite? Share any fond memories associated with bedtime stories. If this wasn't a part of your upbringing, how do you believe it might have impacted you as you matured?

TODAY: In your present life, as you're older, do you believe adults could benefit from reading before bed? Would you consider trying a version of adult bedtime stories if available? If so, what themes would interest you in such stories?

TOMORROW: Envisioning a future with a family and perhaps grandkids, would you read bedtime stories to them? If so, which stories from your childhood would you pass on and why? Beyond the benefits for them, what do you think you would gain from this bonding time?

In the movie *Mary Poppins*, a memorable quote echoes: "Everything is possible, even the impossible." Her words challenge the doubting children to believe in the extraordinary, suggesting the potential for miraculous occurrences. Her quote lends to the whimsical and magical nature of Mary Poppins, inspiring a sense of wonder and a mindset that embraces the limitless possibilities of life.

YESTERDAY: Recall a moment when something seemed impossible until you made it possible. How did you overcome the initial mindset that deemed it unachievable, and did this experience shape your approach to challenges that followed?

TODAY: In your present life, when you face seemingly impossible situations, what is your initial approach? Has your personal growth made dealing with these challenges more feasible over time?

TOMORROW: In the face of situations deemed impossible, some people turn to the belief in miracles. Do you personally believe in miracles, and can you envision a scenario in your future where you might find solace or hope in the idea of a miracle being possible?

A plot twist is a narrative device characterized by an unforeseen and dramatic turn of events, commonly employed in various forms of storytelling such as books, plays, films, and television. Interestingly, our own lives can also be subject to unexpected plot twists that alter the course of our journey.

YESTERDAY: Reflecting on the biggest plot twist in your life thus far, describe what happened and why it caught you off guard. What unfolded in the aftermath, and did this unexpected twist, whether good or bad, leave a lasting impact on your life?

TODAY: Thinking about your present-day life what is the worst plot twist that could happen to you today? What if it did happen, how would you handle it? Who would you lean on to help you navigate this unexpected twist?

TOMORROW: From a writer's perspective, consider your future life and write your own dramatic plot twist (exciting or scary) that could happen. How would you handle this unexpected turn of events if it were to happen?

A person's "happy place" is defined by a location where positive emotions like joy, hope, and happiness are experienced. For many individuals, this place is a sanctuary where they feel carefree, relaxed, and removed from the hassles of life, engaging in activities they love.

YESTERDAY: Taking a look back years ago, where was your happy place? Describe what it was like, how it made you feel and the benefits you got from spending time there.

TODAY: In your current life, describe your happy place. Reflecting on what brings you joy now compared to years ago, identify the significant differences. What does this contrast say about your personal growth and the changes in your life?

TOMORROW: Envisioning your future, if you could design your ideal happy place with any elements you desire, describe what it would be like. Explain the importance of each element in your dream happy place and why they contribute to creating the perfect environment for you.

Traffic signs surround us, each with a specific purpose. Stop signs protect from collisions, detours reroute from potential trouble, and deer crossing prompts a sense of caution. Imagine if life had similar signs, we might navigate through potential hazards more effectively.

YESTERDAY: Reflecting on your past, is there a specific traffic sign whose advice you could have benefited from? Describe the scenario where the guidance of that particular traffic sign would have come in handy.

TODAY: What traffic sign best represents current life? Describe what you chose that sign and why it represents your present circumstances.

TOMORROW: Figuratively, are there specific traffic signs you hope not to encounter in your future, as they might stand in the way of your plans? If so, which signs represent potential obstacles or challenges for you?

Henri Matisse said it best when he said, "Creativity takes courage." This statement reminds us to be bold when it comes to self-expression and to hold nothing back when it comes to sharing our gifts with the world.

YESTERDAY: Reflecting on the past, what was your earliest form of self-expression? How did you discover your creative gifts, and who or what served as your earliest source of inspiration?

TODAY: In your present life, how do you express yourself, and do you agree that creativity takes courage? Additionally, what creative pursuits are you currently engaged in, and how do they add joy to your life?

TOMORROW: How do you think your creative expression will evolve over time as you mature? Are there any unexplored creative passions you have a desire to pursue in the future?

Calgon, a popular water softener and bath powder, elevated the bathing experience to a new level of relaxation, coining their famous slogan, "Calgon, take me away." This phrase became synonymous with the idea of escaping the stresses of daily life.

YESTERDAY: Looking back to a stressful time in your life, what was your "Calgon" equivalent? What helped you escape the stresses of the day?

TODAY: In your present life, what is your favorite way to relax, and how does it differ from years ago? Do you find yourself facing more or fewer stressors currently, and what factors do you attribute to this change? Moreover, are you making sufficient time to decompress and escape from the stresses of your day?

TOMORROW: If you could eliminate one huge stress from your future that is a constant stressor in your life now, what would it be? How would removing this stressor pave the way for a brighter and more positive path forward for you?

Ants, renowned for their strength, have been documented to possess the remarkable ability to carry up to twenty times their own body weight. The secret of an ant's strength lies within their structure.

YESTERDAY: Recall a past instance when you had to dig deep within to summon all your strength to navigate a challenging situation. How did finding the strength to endure impact you, and what noticeable changes did you observe in yourself afterward?

TODAY: Thinking about yourself today, describe your inner, mental and physical strength and how that has changed as you've matured? Who is someone you currently admire for their strength and how to they inspire you?

TOMORROW: Considering your future, do you foresee a time when someone will need to lean on or depend on you for strength? If so, how do you plan to assist them in navigating their situation, and how will you motivate them based on your past experiences of finding strength in tough times?

When Zig Ziglar said, 'People often say that motivation doesn't last. Well, neither does bathing - that's why we recommend it daily,' he used lighthearted humor and a touch of sarcasm to underscore the point that continuous effort is required to seek and maintain motivation.

YESTERDAY: Describe a period in your life where you had zero motivation. How did it affect your mood, appearance and overall quality of life? How did you overcome this phase and are you dealing with any lasting effects from it?

TODAY: What motivates you today? Would you say it's easier or harder to motivate you at this stage in your life as opposed to earlier stages? Explain.

TOMORROW: Envisioning your future, do you believe you will be a good motivator for others? What past experiences have equipped you with motivational insight and abilities, and do you anticipate that being a source of motivation for others will be a rewarding aspect of your life?

Mitchell Clark's quote, "The self-work that you do in silence will echo throughout every part of your life," is a powerful reminder that transformation doesn't always require an audience. The quiet work—the healing, the discipline, the letting go—often goes unnoticed by others but is felt deeply within. When paired with action, this kind of growth becomes undeniable. It strengthens your voice, refines your path, and renders even your harshest critics irrelevant.

YESTERDAY: What inner work have you done—quietly and consistently—that others may never see, but has changed how you show up in the world?

TODAY: In what areas of your life are you still working silently, and how is that shaping your mindset, habits, or self-worth?

TOMORROW: How can you continue to commit to private growth, trusting that the echoes of that effort will resonate long after the noise fades?

Esoteric is a term used to describe a person who is often misunderstood, conveying a sense of mystery or difficulty in understanding. This term also implies an air of secrecy, suggesting that the individual may be considered different from others.

YESTERDAY: Reflecting on your past, were there instances when you felt misunderstood, and did people perceive you as different or mysterious? Describe what that period was like for you and whether it strengthened you or perhaps contributed to developing a complex.

TODAY: In your present self, do you still feel misunderstood, and if so, how? Are there personality aspects or mannerisms you possess that others may find unusual, and do you accept them or stifle them? How can you better embrace your uniqueness in a way that fosters understanding and appreciation from others?

TOMORROW: Thinking ahead to the future, what ways can you use your eccentric traits and experiences from being misunderstood to improve the world around you, and heal a part of yourself in the process?

Becca Lee's words, 'The ocean does not apologize for its depth, and the mountains do not seek forgiveness for the space they take, and so, neither shall I,' aligns with the modern-day unapologetic movement. This movement encourages individuals to embrace their true selves, refusing to conform to society's preconceived notions of who they should be.

YESTERDAY: Reflecting on your past, was there ever a period when you felt the need to pretend to be something you weren't, walk on eggshells, or apologize for being yourself? Recall a time in your life when you had to hide parts of yourself to fit in or conform to an image that wasn't truly reflective of who you are.

TODAY: In your present life, what aspects of your authentic self do you refuse to apologize for? What are the non-negotiable elements of your values and identity that you will never compromise on?

TOMORROW: Envisioning your future, describe what living your best life looks like for you. Paint a picture of your ideal lifestyle and a world that embraces you as you are. Additionally, what steps can you take now to ensure that this vision becomes a reality?

A "potluck dinner" is a communal gathering where everyone invited brings something to the table to share and eat. This concept originates back to the Great Depression era of the 1930s, where food was scarce, and this was an economical way to feed your family. Today potlucks serve to introduce people to each other's cultures and heritage. It's a communal way to appreciate and celebrate others and their traditions.

YESTERDAY: Recall a time when you faced financial struggles, and your budget was limited, similar to the potluck concept designed to support each other during challenging times. How did you pinch pennies and navigate through the tough financial circumstances during that period?

TODAY: Drawing a parallel between a potluck dinner and teamwork, what would you bring to the table in a collaborative setting now? Identify your current strengths and attributes that would be valuable contributions to a team.

TOMORROW: Thinking about your future, if you were to host a potluck for people who wanted to experience parts of your culture, heritage and traditions, what would you serve? Explain what each dish represents and why it is significant to you.

A snake sheds its skin as a necessary part of its evolution, triggered by the fact that the old skin no longer fits and becomes worn out. This process, known as molting, can occur 4-12 times per year. It's a natural reminder that growth often requires releasing what once protected us but can no longer contain who we're becoming.

YESTERDAY: Reflecting on a time when you got serious about pursuing your dreams and set significant goals, what did you recognize that you would have to "shed," similar to a snake shedding its skin, in order to evolve into the person you aspired to become?

TODAY: Examining your current life and considering the things you want to achieve, what no longer fits in the picture you've outlined in your mind? Additionally, when it comes to the evolution process and taking the next step in your growth or elevation, what do you find to be the most challenging part?

TOMORROW: Anticipating the future you aim to create, what do you foresee yourself outgrowing? Will there be people, habits, or even a lifestyle that might be detrimental to reaching your desired destination?

"Be kind," "spread kindness," and "choose kindness" are all expressions encouraging individuals to act kindly in a world where many may not. The underlying message of the kindness movement is that kindness is free and costs nothing, yet the world greatly benefits from it.

YESTERDAY: Reflecting on your earlier years, were you naturally kind, or was kindness something you were taught that inspired you to pay it forward? Additionally, has someone ever shown you an act of kindness that made a lasting impression, and if so, what did they do?

TODAY: In your present life, how do you currently spread kindness? Do you believe that being kind to others plays a role in your mental well-being?

TOMORROW: Envisioning your future and considering the example you may want to set for your children or to contribute to making the world a better place, what acts of kindness do you plan to continue? Furthermore, which acts of kindness do you believe will make the most significant impact for the direction in which the world is headed?

"Let it Go" is a popular song from the Disney animated film "Frozen." The lyrics convey the message of letting go of fear, anger, and negative emotions, while embracing self-acceptance and the importance of individuality.

YESTERDAY: Reflecting on past struggles that may have been exacerbated by your difficulty in letting certain things go, how could you have improved this situation in hindsight? What negative emotions and mindset contributed to making it more complicated than necessary?

TODAY: In your present daily life, what do you find you need to remind yourself to let go of? Are there lingering negative emotions that still impact you and contribute to heightening certain situations?

TOMORROW: If you were to speak to or counsel a group of people, especially teenagers, wrestling with similar issues and emotions they find challenging to let go of, what words of encouragement would you offer? Additionally, is there a specific example from your past that could serve as a valuable lesson for someone facing similar struggles in the future?

The Statue of Liberty, standing tall in New York Harbor, is not only an iconic symbol of the United States but also embodies the core principles that the nation cherishes. This colossal statue, a gift from France in 1886, has become a universal emblem of freedom and democracy.

YESTERDAY: Reflecting on your past, can you describe a moment when you first experienced a sense of freedom? Was it tied to your first job, obtaining a car, or perhaps having an extended curfew? How liberating did this newfound freedom make you feel?

TODAY: In your present life, what makes you feel free and grants you a sense of independence? How does this feeling differ now that you're older compared to your younger self? Do you think that more freedom comes with increased responsibility?

TOMORROW: Dreaming ahead to an ideal future where you are completely independent from your current constraints and obligations, can you describe what that looks like? Additionally, do you believe there is such a thing as having too much freedom?

The saying, "Laughter is the best medicine," isn't just a metaphor; it holds profound truth. Scientifically proven to reduce stress, promote happiness, and offer various physical health benefits, laughter is a universal language that strengthens social bonds and develops positive relationships.

YESTERDAY: Reminisce about a person from your past who always made you laugh? What made them funny and what did it feel like when they were around? Are you still in touch with them?

TODAY: In your current life, who makes you laugh? Describe your sense of humor and your perception of how funny you think you are. Additionally, how would your friends and family describe your sense of humor?

TOMORROW: If you were to perform a stand-up comedy routine a year from now, what material from your life would you use to make others laugh? What people, incidents, or encounters do you think would contribute to a great and entertaining show?

"Actions speak louder than words" is not just a saying; it's a powerful call to action. This proverb underscores the significance of backing up spoken promises with tangible deeds. Mere words can be empty without corresponding actions, and this dichotomy often calls one's character into question.

YESTERDAY: Recall a time in your past when you promised to do something for someone and didn't follow through, or vice versa. What emotions were involved, and did it result in a loss of trust or damage to the relationship?

TODAY: In your present life, if you had to deal with someone who consistently promised things but never backed it up with action, how would you handle the situation? What approach would you take to address the issue and maintain a healthy relationship?

TOMORROW: Envisioning tomorrow, have you made promises to someone or committed to doing something that is approaching, and you haven't fulfilled it yet? What steps can you take now to ensure that it gets done in the future?

The phrases "life isn't fair," "dog eat dog world," and "only the strong survive" all serve as similar reminders that life can be tough, and circumstances may not always be fair. This trio of expressions conveys the harsh realities of life, emphasizing the idea that challenges and competition are inherent in the journey. It's akin to the advice to "buckle up" when embarking on life's unpredictable ride.

YESTERDAY: Recall the first time you had an encounter that made you think life wasn't fair. What happened, and who did you turn to for help or advice? What was the result or resolution?

TODAY: In your present perspective, do you feel that life, in general, is unfair, or do you perceive certain aspects of life as unfair? Elaborate on your thoughts and how you navigate these feelings in your current life.

TOMORROW: Contemplating your future, what steps can you take now to make life fairer for yourself and your family? Do you believe succumbing to a victim mindset could hinder your ability to dream bigger? Additionally, are there future aspirations you have that this mindset might interfere with, and how can you overcome it to achieve your goals?

A marathon is a grueling long-distance foot race that tests an individual's physical and mental strength and endurance. The Boston Marathon, recognized as the world's oldest annual marathon, holds a prestigious status among road racing events globally.

YESTERDAY: Reflect on a time in your life when it felt like you were racing through everything, moving so fast that you didn't stop to smell the roses or enjoy the small things. In hindsight, what do you think you may have missed out on during that period?

TODAY: In your current life, what feels like a marathon, a race that seems never-ending? Moreover, what strategies or factors help you maintain endurance and keep pushing forward?

TOMORROW: Considering your future from a race perspective, what do you envision as your finish line? What dream or goal keeps you motivated and propels you forward in the race of life?

Friendship bread is initiated with a dough starter comprised of water, flour, milk, sugar, and yeast, similar to a sourdough. The starter, a living entity, requires care and cultivation. Its origins trace back to the 1860s when pioneer women shared it during their long journeys. During the Great Depression, the Amish crafted their version, generously distributing it within their community, particularly to the sick and needy.

YESTERDAY: Recall the time when you met your best friend or a close friend. Did you have anything that symbolized your friendship, such as a bracelet or tattoo? What did this friendship mean to you during that period?

TODAY: Considering your current friends, if one of them fell sick or faced hard times, what actions or support would you provide that symbolize the friendship bread of the Depression era?

TOMORROW: Looking ahead, what future plans have you and your friends made? Are there specific activities or adventures you plan to embark on that will further strengthen the bonds of your friendship?

“Shout” is a song by the iconic 80s band Tears for Fears. The lyrics, “Shout, shout, let it all out,” encapsulate the song’s tone and message. It encourages rebellion against perceived injustice, emphasizes the importance of using one’s voice, and promotes the idea of not suppressing emotions during stressful times, and views shouting as a cathartic release.

YESTERDAY: Describe a time from your past where you either experienced or witnessed an injustice. How did it make you feel, what did it motivate you to do, and did it shape your dreams?

TODAY: If you were to rebel against something today to contribute to a better tomorrow, what would it be, and why is it important to you? Describe the cause or issue that you feel strongly about and want to take a stand against.

TOMORROW: Conceptualize an ideal future society. What does it look like to you? Envision a world where certain injustices no longer exist, fostering a harmonious and equitable existence. Describe the key aspects and changes that contribute to this vision.

Bruce Lee's mindful quote, "If you love life, don't waste time, for time is what life is made up of," underscores the profound value of time, emphasizing that it is more precious than money.

YESTERDAY: Reflecting on your past, do you feel like you wasted a significant amount of time? Did you value your time, or did you align with the motto "time you enjoyed wasting wasn't wasted"? If given the chance to reclaim some of the time you spent, what would you use it for instead?

TODAY: In your present life, how valuable is your time? What activities occupy most of your day, and is there something you feel you never have enough time for? Have you considered eliminating certain tasks or commitments that consume too much time to make room for activities that bring you more fulfillment and joy?

TOMORROW: Envisioning your future years, how do you hope to spend the majority of your time? What do you anticipate being the most important aspect of your life during that stage, and what changes or adjustments do you think you'll need to make to ensure that priority is fulfilled?

The metamorphosis process in butterflies is a profound journey that symbolizes transformation and hope. Beginning as a humble caterpillar, it undergoes a remarkable transition, ultimately emerging as an exquisite, beautiful winged creature. The cycle transcends its biological significance and serves as a powerful metaphor for rebirth and resurrection.

YESTERDAY: Reflect on a time from your past when you underwent a significant transformation or rebirth. What was the most substantial change, and how did your life differ afterward? Describe the impact this transformation had on your overall well-being and experiences.

TODAY: Reflect on the changes and growth you've undergone, and how they resemble the transformative process of a butterfly. When you look at your past compared to where you are today, what aspects of your journey remind you of their rebirth?

TOMORROW: Considering the future, what transformations or changes are you planning for yourself, your career, or your life in general? Why do you feel these changes or transitions are necessary, and are they driven by a desire to fulfill a dream or address something that feels lacking in your life?

"Don't let the sun go down on your anger" is a proverb with roots in biblical teachings. This metaphorical expression advises against letting anger linger without reflection or resolution. Rather than hastily suppressing or expressing anger, it encourages individuals to process and contemplate their emotions.

YESTERDAY: Recall an incident from your past where your temper got the best of you, leading to a negative result that deeply impacted your life. What did you learn about yourself during that time, and how did this experience shape your understanding of managing emotions?

TODAY: In your present life, when you find yourself losing your temper, do you tend to act impulsively without thinking, or do you give yourself time to process how you feel? Are you quick to anger, or does it take a lot to upset you? Reflect on your current approach to managing emotions in heated situations.

TOMORROW: Looking ahead to your future, what goals do you have concerning your overall mental health and well-being? What specific aspects of managing your emotions and reactions do you plan on working on to reach the desired state of control and balance in your life?

Walking or taking a trip "Down memory lane" is an idiom that refers to revisiting or reminiscing about past events, experiences, or memories. It's often used to evoke nostalgia or to reflect on the passage of time, allowing individuals to cherish and reflect upon moments from days gone by.

YESTERDAY: Reflecting on past memories, which one is your favorite and makes taking a trip down memory lane worthwhile? How does this memory make you feel, and what aspects of it do you cherish the most?

TODAY: In your present life, what specific things or experiences spark nostalgic memories for you? Describe these triggers and the memories associated with each item or experience that brings forth a sense of nostalgia.

TOMORROW: Anticipating your future, what memories do you hope to create? Who would you like to be a part of these memories, and what significance will these future experiences hold for you? Envision the type of moments you aspire to cherish in the days to come.

The well-known phrase "forgive and forget" suggests that one should not only forgive others for hurting them but also strive to forget the wrongdoing, emphasizing the importance of letting go of grudges and moving forward with a clean slate.

YESTERDAY: Recall a moment from your past when someone hurt you. What transpired, and did the person responsible ask for your forgiveness? If they did, how did you respond, and were you able to find it within yourself to forgive them?

TODAY: In your present life, do you need to ask someone for forgiveness or forgive someone else? Reflect on what you've learned about forgiveness over the years and how it shapes your current outlook on seeking or offering forgiveness.

TOMORROW: Contemplating your future, is there someone you've forgiven but still struggle to forget what they've done? Reflect on what it would mean for your future if you could let go of dwelling on that negative moment and move forward with a sense of closure.

Buddha's words, "Three things cannot be long hidden: the sun, the moon, and the truth," carry a profound message about the inevitability of truth and the persistence of hidden realities. The analogy underscores the idea that, in the end, truth will always emerge, much like the unyielding presence of the sun and the moon in the sky.

YESTERDAY: Recall a past instance when you lied to someone and the truth came out. How did you feel in the moment your lie was exposed, and did this experience make you more inclined to prioritize honesty in your interactions?

TODAY: In your current life, how do you handle situations when someone lies to you? Additionally, how easy is it for you to detect when someone is being untruthful?

TOMORROW: Looking ahead, are you waiting for a lie to be exposed in your future? If so, consider whether there's anything you can proactively do now to address the situation or speed up the process.

The saying "beauty is only skin-deep" is more than just a phrase; it's a lesson. It conveys the idea that while someone may be beautiful on the outside, if their character—what's inside—is flawed or negative, their attractiveness diminishes.

YESTERDAY: Reflecting on your past years, what was your concept of beauty? What factors influenced your perception of beauty, and did you ever form any unhealthy ideals related to superficial beauty?

TODAY: In your present perspective, what is your idea of beauty, and how does it differ from your views in the past? Additionally, describe the aspects of yourself that you consider beautiful, extending beyond just the physical attributes.

TOMORROW: Looking ahead to the future and the aging process, do you have any fears or concerns that you need to work through regarding getting older? Consider what steps you can take now to foster an appreciation for the later stages of your life.

Reality television became a popular niche genre in the early 90s with shows such as *The Real World*. It took off and exploded in the early 2000s with the success of series like *Survivor, American Idol,* and *Big Brother*, all of which became global franchises.

YESTERDAY: Recall your earliest introduction to reality TV. What were your initial thoughts about it? Did it resonate with you, and if so, what specific aspects did you like about reality TV?

TODAY: If your life was filmed presently from a reality show standpoint, what would keep the audience entertained? Is there any part of your life that would be off limits or are you all in?

TOMORROW: If you could script your own reality TV show for your life in the future, what would the highlights look like? What things would you add to the script that are not currently part of your life?

"I hope you never lose your sense of wonder; you get your fill to eat but always keep that hunger," are lyrics from the Lee Ann Womack song "I Hope You Dance." Her life-affirming song carries an uplifting and timeless message. It is narrated from the perspective of a mother expressing her wish that her children embrace life, take chances on love and faith, and maintain a sense of wonder.

YESTERDAY: Reflecting on your younger years, what hopes and dreams did your parents have for your life? Can you recall if they shared aspirations that resonated with the sentiments expressed in Lee Ann Womack's song lyrics?

TODAY: Considering the title of the song "I Hope You Dance," how would you say you're dancing in your life now? What actions are you taking to maintain a sense of wonder, and what chances or risks are you presently embracing?

TOMORROW: Anticipating your future, what hopes and dreams do you envision having for your children? How do you plan to support and encourage them in their journey to dance through life in their unique way?

"Advice from a Frog" takes the playful and symbolic nature of frogs to offer life advice. The phrases incorporate frog-related behaviors and characteristics into a set of whimsical suggestions: Make a splash, look before you leap, don't jump to conclusions, enjoy a good swim, stretch your legs often, spend time at your pad, and hop to it!

YESTERDAY: Taking into consideration all the advice from a frog, which one was a struggle for you in the past? Why do you think it was a struggle and is it something you're still working on?

TODAY: Reflecting on the frog's advice to "stretch your legs," how are you applying that in your current life? Can you describe how this advice translates into your present-day actions and endeavors?

TOMORROW: Looking ahead, again keeping with the frog's advice, "make a splash," how will you do that in the future? What have you been thinking about recently that could constitute making a splash tomorrow?

"Roll out the welcome mat" is an expression that signifies extending a warm welcome or being hospitable. The phrase originates from the common practice of placing welcome mats in front of homes as a symbol of good will and hospitality.

YESTERDAY: Reflect on a past moment when you felt genuinely welcomed by someone, describe the details of that situation and how it impacted your approach to welcoming others.

TODAY: Thinking about your present life, do you roll out the welcome mat for people? Do you like visitors, entertaining and having people at your home? How do you create a welcoming atmosphere for visitors in your present life?

TOMORROW: Do you anticipate traveling or visiting somewhere in the future where you worry about being welcomed? What reservations do you have about going and why do you worry you won't be welcomed?

A "bucket list" is essentially a compilation of aspirations and accomplishments that an individual desires to achieve or experience throughout their lifetime. This term stems from the notion of creating a list of goals before one "kicks the bucket," a colloquial expression for passing away.

YESTERDAY: Think back to the first time you heard the expression "bucket list." What were your initial thoughts and how did it influence the way you saw life?

TODAY: In your present life, do you find the concept of a "bucket list" meaningful, or do you prefer to approach life's experiences without the pressure of a predefined list?

TOMORROW: In the future, should you choose to create a "bucket list" what are a few things that would be on this list and why are they meaningful to you?

The phrase "it's never too late to teach an old dog new tricks" is an expression conveying the idea that individuals, regardless of age, can still learn and adapt to new things or acquire new skills. It emphasizes the potential for growth and change, even in those who are considered "set in their ways."

YESTERDAY: When you were younger, how did you perceive older people? Did you dismiss them, or did you find value and wisdom in their life stories and lessons?

TODAY: Currently, are you set in your ways when it comes to certain things? Do you have a routine or habit that gives you a sense of comfort but keeps you from exploring new possibilities?

TOMORROW: Regarding your future as you begin to mature and thinking about the phrase "it's never too late to teach an old dogs new tricks," do you think you will be open to trying new things or keeping up with trends and technology and continue to learn or do you think you will have other priorities?

The metaphor "Life is a rollercoaster" suggests that life is filled with highs and lows, just like the exhilarating and unpredictable experience of riding a roller coaster. This comparison highlights the dynamic and unpredictable nature of life, with moments of excitement, fear, and unexpected twists and turns.

YESTERDAY: Recall a time from your past when life felt like a rollercoaster. How did you cope with the ups and downs, and what strategies helped you navigate through it?

TODAY: Thinking about your life now, what part of your day feels like a rollercoaster? Is there anything you can do to make your day smoother?

TOMORROW: Looking ahead, what aspects or experiences are you hoping will bring excitement and exhilaration to your future, like the thrill of a rollercoaster ride?

Wayne Dyer's quote, "Judging a person does not define who they are. It defines who you are," emphasizes the significance of refraining from making assumptions about others, highlighting that judgments reveal more about the person making them.

YESTERDAY: Describe a time from your past when you made judgments about another person. What happened, how did you make them feel, and how did you feel? Did you learn anything about judging others?

TODAY: Do you find others judging you presently, and if so, what assumptions do they make about you? How does this make you feel and has it changed the way you view others?

TOMORROW: Looking ahead to your future, what will you teach your children about judging others? What experiences will you share with them?

There's a powerful quote of unknown origin that says, "Heritage is a present from our ancestors; respect it, preserve it." Passing down traditions from one generation to the next is a perfect example of this sentiment.

YESTERDAY: What was the first family tradition introduced to you, and how did it shape your understanding of family values and connections? Describe the emotions and significance associated with learning about this tradition.

TODAY: Presently, what traditions are you continuing your family taught you, and what new traditions have you created on your own?

TOMORROW: In the future, what additional aspects of your heritage do you wish to explore further? Are you considering a trip to visit your family's origin or the land of your ancestors? What insights do you hope to gain from such an experience?

Talent competitions have been around for decades. Though they have evolved over time the premise is still the same, bringing to light hidden talents in individuals, and discovering untapped potential.

YESTERDAY: Thinking back when was the first time you discovered one of your talents? How did you discover it, and did you continue to nurture it? What impact did the discovery of your talent have on your life? Did it lead you to pursue new opportunities or shape your identity in a significant way?

TODAY: What are you doing with your talents currently? Have you discovered any new talents and what role does your talent play in your everyday life?

TOMORROW: Considering your strongest talent and looking to your future, do you see anything blossoming or happening with this talent? What would be your dream scenario?

A hot air balloon is a great way to look at the land from an aerial view. It gives you a different perspective allowing you to see common surroundings in a whole new way. If only we would treat life like a hot air balloon and take advantage of new perspectives, we may have a different view on certain things.

YESTERDAY: Think back to a situation where having a different perspective would have been beneficial. What new possibilities could it have opened your mind to and allowed you to see the issue from another viewpoint?

TODAY: Think about a decision you made today; did you consider all the angles, and did you take the time to look at it from a different perspective? If you reexamine your decision and think about it with those questions in mind, would the outcome be different?

TOMORROW: Facing future decisions, imagine exploring possibilities from the viewpoint of a hot air balloon. Allow your mind to open to unconventional perspectives, fostering creativity and uncovering novel ideas in the process. Write a list of new possibilities concerning these future decisions.

There's a lesson to be learned in the game "tug of war," and though it feels like it's only a test of strength, the importance of working together is clear. Teamwork is about embracing a common purpose, exceeding our limits, and finding inspiration in each other. The analogy between tug of war and teamwork is congruent.

YESTERDAY: Have you ever played "tug of war" and if so, did you learn anything from the experience? Would you play it again, why or why not?

TODAY: Thinking of your present-day job, do you prefer working independently or in a team setting? Explain.

TOMORROW: Thinking about your future through the lens of the game "tug of war," what have you learned about give and take, teamwork, and exceeding your limits that can help you on your future road of life?

While social media often attempts to frame "toxic traits" as lighthearted jokes, it's crucial to recognize that these traits are genuine. If left unaddressed, such behaviors can result in consequences, particularly by alienating those around you. A "toxic trait" refers to a negative habit or behavior that may pose harm to oneself or others.

YESTERDAY: Reflecting on the past, did you have a recurring "toxic trait," and if so, who pointed it out to you, and how did you address and overcome it?

TODAY: Presently, what toxic trait do you find the hardest to deal with in others? If you should happen to encounter someone with this trait, how do you handle it?

TOMORROW: What toxic trait are you still working on that you worry about affecting your future negatively? What help are you getting now that you hope will pay off later?

Chameleons, have the fascinating ability to make intricate color adjustments, and showcase a remarkable adaptation to their environment. Beyond mere camouflage, their mood intricately mirrors their reactions to their ever-changing surroundings. As humans, there's a profound lesson to be learned from their capacity to seamlessly blend in and adapt.

YESTERDAY: Share a past situation where you had to adapt to overcome challenges. What adjustments did you make, and how did they help you navigate through that difficult time?

TODAY: Reflect on how you act like a chameleon in your current life—consider the adjustments you make to blend into your environment and the aspects you might camouflage to conceal details you prefer not to be noticed.

TOMORROW: What lessons have you learned about blending in and adapting that will help you successfully navigate an upcoming challenge in your future?

Within the rich tapestry of Celtic mythology, the unicorn stands as a captivating symbol, distinguished by its ethereal white horse-like form and a singular, spiraling horn. This mythical creature transcends mere physical attributes, becoming a profound representation of purity, innocence, and formidable power.

YESTERDAY: When you first saw a unicorn what were your initial thoughts? What feelings did it evoke and what did it represent to you?

TODAY: Consider your current life and describe any commonalities you find with a unicorn. What unique or magical aspects do you identify in your present circumstances?

TOMORROW: Looking ahead to your future, what do you hope will be captivating and add a touch of mystique, like the enchantment associated with a unicorn?

Kate Spencer's quote, "Intuition is your soul whispering the truth to your heart and hoping that you hear," beautifully underscores the significance of intuition. It highlights the importance of tuning in to that internal voice, often dismissed, which carries profound insights.

YESTERDAY: Reflect on a moment when you had a strong intuition but chose to ignore it. What unfolded as a result of not following your gut, and what valuable lesson did you learn from that experience?

TODAY: In your current day-to-day life, do you trust and follow your instincts and intuition? Reflect on how your intuition has evolved as you've matured, and do you feel it's stronger now compared to the past?

TOMORROW: Consider an upcoming scenario in your future where you might be wholly dependent on your instincts. What specific aspects are you hoping your gut will guide you through in that situation?

Rihanna's "Diamonds" transcends being merely a song; it stands as an anthem, a wellspring of inspiration, and a mindset that reinforces the notion that diamonds are forged under pressure. The opening line, "Shine bright like a diamond," encapsulates not just a musical lyric but a powerful mantra. It serves as a poignant reminder to never allow the world to dim your radiant glow.

YESTERDAY: Revisit a past moment when you faced a highly stressful situation, like the pressure a diamond undergoes. How did this experience shape you, and do you believe you emerged stronger or better for having gone through it?

TODAY: In your present life, how are you shining bright like a diamond? What things or circumstances try to dull your shine and how do you handle them?

TOMORROW: Using past experiences as a guide, create an inspirational mantra reflecting the strength of a diamond, serving as a source of empowerment for the future.

The term "calling an audible" originates from American Football, describing a scenario where the quarterback alters the play last-minute based on the defense's positioning. Life, in a similar fashion, could benefit from adopting this strategy. Embracing flexibility in our plans and, much like calling an audible in football, adjusting when something doesn't look or feel right can be a valuable approach.

YESTERDAY: Think back to a time when something you were looking forward to didn't go as planned. Did you allow this surprise to frustrate you or were you able to recover? What did you learn about yourself through that event?

TODAY: How flexible are you presently when it comes to your plans? Do you get easily frustrated or upset when things don't go the way you planned? How can you increase your flexibility when it comes to strategy?

TOMORROW: Think about a future milestone or life event you plan on celebrating. What if something doesn't go the way you planned and you have to make adjustments or call an audible? Create alternate solutions you can have handy in case you need to make changes.

The expression "recharge your batteries" is used when individuals need to step back from work or specific activities to rest and rejuvenate. This practice serves as a valuable method to prevent burnout, providing a necessary break for both the mind and body when fatigue sets in.

YESTERDAY: Recall a period in your life when you were doing too much and not resting enough. How did you end up in that situation, what happened to you and how did you recover?

TODAY: Presently, what drains your battery the fastest, what sucks the most energy out of you? What can you do to ensure you're making time to recharge your battery? Additionally, how can you eliminate things that could potentially lead to burn out?

TOMORROW: Thinking ahead to all the things you have planned for your future, write down some new and relaxing ideas for recharging your battery. What specific mistakes do you want to avoid in the future that you've made in the past in this area?

"Burning bridges" encapsulates a metaphorical act that goes beyond mere separation; it symbolizes the deliberate and often irreparable destruction or damage to a relationship or connection. This expression implies a significant and consequential decision, suggesting that the ties between individuals have been severed in a way that makes reconciliation difficult, if not impossible.

YESTERDAY: Think about a time where you burned a bridge. How did it happen, and do you regret it and if you could go back and change things would you?

TODAY: How do you handle it when people burn a bridge with you today? Are you more sympathetic and inclined to extend an opportunity to rebuild that bridge, or do you typically leave it burnt? What shapes your outlook on this, and does it relate to past experiences?

TOMORROW: Thinking about your future, what bridge in your life is important that you would protect it at all costs? Why do you value this relationship and why is it important to your path forward?

Adele's song "Chasing Pavements" delves into the theme of pursuing something that ultimately leads to nowhere, whether it be a relationship, a dead-end job, or an unattainable dream. The poignant line, "Should I give up or should I just keep chasing pavements even if it leads nowhere," references the internal struggle many individuals face at some point in their lives.

YESTERDAY: Recall a time you pursued something that led nowhere. What did you feel and what prompted you to pursue it? Where did you hope it would lead?

TODAY: Based on past experience are you more conscientious of your pursuits currently? How do you determine in your current life if something or someone is worth pursuing?

TOMORROW: Thinking about your future, what have you been contemplating pursuing for a long time that you're working on the courage to go after it? Do you have any apprehensions?

When kids wanted to do something their parents or teachers didn't like, they may have heard the question, "If everyone else jumped off a bridge, would you?" The underlying wisdom is a caution against blindly following the crowd, emphasizing the importance of independent thinking. This age-old logic encourages individuals to make decisions based on personal judgment rather than succumbing to peer pressure.

YESTERDAY: Think about a time from your past where you fell victim to peer pressure. What happened and were there any consequences? Did this make you think twice when confronted with peer pressure again?

TODAY: Thinking about yourself today, do you tend to follow the crowd, or do you go your own way? In your opinion, what are the pros and cons of each scenario?

TOMORROW: Looking ahead, if you have children, and they want to do something their friends are doing but you won't allow it, what will you say to them? How will you approach this situation?

The phrase "Started from the bottom now we're here," made iconic by rapper Drake, became a modern-day declaration of perseverance and resilience. More than a lyric, it echoed the emotional and personal grind behind success, often unrecognized by the outside world. For many, this phrase isn't just about material growth—it's about emotional, spiritual, and personal evolution from a place of struggle to a place of strength.

YESTERDAY: What did "the bottom" look like for you? Reflect on a time in your past where you felt stuck, overlooked, or lost.

TODAY: Where are you now in relation to that starting point? What milestones or shifts have marked your progress?

TOMORROW: Looking forward, what will "we're here" mean for your future self? How will you define your next level of growth?

The saying "You can't pour from an empty cup" has become a guiding mantra in conversations about burnout, boundaries, and self-care. While often shared casually, its meaning cuts deep—reminding us that giving to others requires first giving to ourselves. The metaphor of the empty cup resonates with anyone who has stretched themselves too thin while ignoring their own needs.

YESTERDAY: Recall a time in your past when you poured too much into others and neglected your own well-being. What did that teach you?

TODAY: How do you protect your energy now, and what does filling your own cup look like in practice?

TOMORROW: In your future, what habits or boundaries will help you live with more balance and emotional sustainability?

The lyric "Just keep swimming," made famous by Dory in *Finding Nemo*, is deceptively simple. Spoken by a forgetful but determined fish, it became a symbol of enduring hope through uncertainty. Behind its cheerfulness is a message of persistence—of moving forward even when the path is unclear, and trusting that action itself is sometimes enough.

YESTERDAY: Think back to a time when you kept going despite feeling uncertain or overwhelmed. What kept you moving?

TODAY: What are you swimming through now? Where are you learning to trust the process rather than the plan?

TOMORROW: What does perseverance look like for the person you are becoming, and what would you like to remember when things get hard?

The widely shared affirmation "You are enough" has become a powerful response to a world that often tells us we must earn worthiness through achievement or perfection. Though short and simple, the phrase has sparked emotional healing and deep reflection for many—serving as a reminder that value is not something to chase, but something inherent.

YESTERDAY: When was the first time you questioned your worth? What external voices shaped that feeling?

TODAY: How are you reclaiming your sense of enough-ness in your current life? What helps reinforce it now?

TOMORROW: Imagine a future where you live completely aligned with the belief that you are enough—how would that change the way you move through life?

The phrase "May the odds be ever in your favor", popularized by *The Hunger Games* series, has come to represent more than fictional dystopia. It's become a commentary on the moments in life where the stakes feel high and the outcome uncertain. Whether navigating hardship, transition, or risk—it asks us to reflect on how much of life is within our control, and how much we face with courage despite the unknown.

YESTERDAY: Write about a time when you took a risk or faced difficult odds. What did you learn from the experience?

TODAY: Where in your life are you currently hoping for strength, clarity, or a favorable outcome?

TOMORROW: How do you want to face future challenges? What would it look like to trust yourself more than the odds?

The lyric "It was all a dream," famously opens The Notorious B.I.G.'s "Juicy," a track that became an anthem for transformation. For many, the idea that life can shift from imagined possibility to lived reality speaks to the power of perseverance, vision, and self-belief. What once felt far away often becomes the very life we step into—with time, intention, and growth.

YESTERDAY: Think about a dream you once had that felt unrealistic or unreachable. Where did that dream come from, and what did it mean to you at the time?

TODAY: What dreams have become part of your reality? How did you make them real—or why did they change?

TOMORROW: What new dream are you planting seeds for, even if it feels far off now?

The internet phrase "You glow differently when…" began as a way to describe inner change that shows up on the outside. Whether after healing, leaving a toxic space, or reconnecting with joy, the glow is never just physical—it's a reflection of alignment, energy, and self-worth. It's a subtle transformation that others feel even before you fully see it in yourself.

YESTERDAY: Reflect on a time in your life when you felt dimmed—emotionally, spiritually, or energetically. What dulled your inner glow?

TODAY: What makes you glow differently now? What has changed or healed that others might sense in you?

TOMORROW: What would glowing look like in the future? What needs to stay or shift for that light to remain steady?

“Understood the assignment,” a phrase that quickly became part of internet lingo, is now used to describe someone who not only shows up—but shows up with excellence, intention, or authenticity. It’s become a cultural nod to knowing your role, purpose, or moment—and owning it completely.

YESTERDAY: Write about a time in your past when you rose to a challenge or fulfilled a purpose in a way that surprised even you.

TODAY: What “assignments” are you navigating now in your life—roles, responsibilities, or emotional tasks?

TOMORROW: Looking ahead, what assignment do you hope to be ready for? What would showing up fully look like?

"You deserve a soft life," is more than a social media trend—it's a powerful reframing. For those taught to survive instead of thrive, softness can feel radical. The phrase challenges hustle culture, emotional repression, and the belief that rest must be earned. It invites us to believe that ease, peace, and gentleness are not luxuries, but rights.

YESTERDAY: Reflect on how you were taught to relate to rest, softness, and ease. Did it feel safe or selfish?

TODAY: How are you allowing more softness in your life now? What do you still resist?

TOMORROW: Imagine your future living a soft life. What does it look like in practice—not just feeling, but daily rhythm?

The lyric "You're on your own, kid," from Taylor Swift's Midnights album, struck a deep chord with listeners navigating change, growing up, or facing life-defining independence. It's not just about solitude—it's about the bittersweet power of becoming independent.

YESTERDAY: When did you first realize you had to rely on yourself? How did that moment shape you?

TODAY: What are you currently facing alone, and how are you supporting yourself through it?

TOMORROW: What does self-reliance look like for your future self, and how will you continue to grow from it?

The quote "Comparison is the thief of joy," often attributed to Theodore Roosevelt, remains one of the most resonant reflections on modern life. In a world of curated images and constant updates, measuring ourselves against others is both common and damaging. This phrase serves as a reminder to return to our own timeline.

YESTERDAY: Think about a time in your life when comparison overshadowed your progress or peace. What did you learn from that season?

TODAY: How do you handle comparison now? What practices or mindsets help you stay grounded in your own journey?

TOMORROW: In the future, how do you plan to honor your growth without letting others' paths interfere?

"Main character energy" has become a popular way to describe someone fully embracing their identity, choices, and narrative—living as the lead in their own story rather than a background character in someone else's. It's a phrase rooted in reclamation and confidence.

YESTERDAY: When did you first feel like a supporting role in your own life? What circumstances or beliefs kept you small?

TODAY: Where are you stepping into main character energy now? What scenes or chapters are you owning?

TOMORROW: Imagine a version of you who boldly writes and stars in their own future. What story are you telling?

The phrase "Protect your peace" has become a modern mental wellness mantra. It's a call to honor boundaries, energy, and emotional health above the noise. In a world that often demands too much, protecting your peace becomes an act of radical self-respect.

YESTERDAY: Reflect on a time you sacrificed peace for acceptance, success, or someone else's comfort.

TODAY: How do you protect your peace now—and what do you still struggle to say no to?

TOMORROW: What kind of boundaries, routines, or people will support your peace in the future?

The phrase "Let that sink in," often used online to emphasize a truth or realization, has grown beyond its meme roots. In a world that moves fast, it reminds us to pause—really pause—and allow insights to settle before reacting or moving on.

YESTERDAY: Recall a moment from your past that only made sense with time. What finally sank in?

TODAY: What truth or realization are you sitting with right now?

TOMORROW: What insight do you want to carry with you, giving it time and space to deepen in the years ahead?

The phrase "Heavy is the head that wears the crown" reflects the emotional burden of leadership, responsibility, or visibility. Originally from Shakespeare, it's echoed through rap lyrics, modern culture, and motivational talk alike. It speaks to the unseen weight of roles that seem strong on the outside.

YESTERDAY: Think of a time when you were expected to be strong. What did that weight feel like?

TODAY: Where do you carry invisible pressure or responsibility now?

TOMORROW: How will you continue to lead or care for others while also protecting your own well-being?

The quote "Your future self is watching you through memories," shared widely online, offers a poetic reminder that the choices we make today become the moments we'll one day reflect on. It places us directly between reflection and creation.

YESTERDAY: Think about a version of your past self. What do you think they hoped you'd become?

TODAY: What memory are you currently creating for your future self to look back on?

TOMORROW: What do you hope your future self remembers about this season of your life?

The phrase "This too shall pass" has been used for generations to offer comfort during hard times. Its quiet wisdom lies in its dual meaning: joy passes, pain passes—everything evolves. It asks us to meet the present moment with presence, not permanence.

YESTERDAY: Recall a season of life that felt like it would never end. What changed?

TODAY: What challenge or joy are you holding now, knowing it too will pass?

TOMORROW: How can you remind yourself that change is constant, and that no feeling is final?

The lyric "You can't always get what you want," made famous by The Rolling Stones, became an anthem of reluctant acceptance. But the second half—"but if you try sometimes, you just might find, you get what you need"—reminds us that life often provides, just not in the way we expect.

YESTERDAY: Think of a time when you didn't get what you wanted. What did you receive instead?

TODAY: What needs are being met in your life right now, even if they don't look how you imagined?

TOMORROW: How can you open yourself to receive what's truly needed, even when it challenges your plans?

"You've got mail!" was once the most exciting sound of the early internet era, promising connection and new possibilities. Technology may have evolved, but the longing for meaningful communication hasn't changed.

YESTERDAY: What forms of connection meant the most to you growing up?

TODAY: How do you maintain meaningful communication in a digital world?

TOMORROW: What kind of connection—emotional, personal, or creative—do you hope to build more of?

In the world of *Sesame Street*, simple characters delivered lifelong lessons. One of the most beloved was Cookie Monster—whose unfiltered hunger became a symbol of joy, impulse, and incorrigible desire. Underneath the silliness was a deeper lesson: sometimes we suppress what we want because we've been taught it's "too much."

YESTERDAY: What was something you were told to quiet or hide about yourself as a child?

TODAY: Where in your life are you still denying or controlling a natural craving or want?

TOMORROW: What would it look like to pursue joy or pleasure—without guilt, just like Cookie?

In *Toy Story,* the character Buzz Lightyear begins his journey believing he's a real space ranger, only to discover he's a toy. The heartbreak is real—but so is the transformation. In learning the truth, he finds greater meaning and connection. It's a powerful metaphor for identity, illusion, and growth.

YESTERDAY: What part of your identity once felt real but turned out to be an illusion?

TODAY: How are you defining who you are now—based on reality, not fantasy or expectation?

TOMORROW: What part of your story are you ready to reframe with more honesty and heart?

Brené Brown once said, "Vulnerability is not winning or losing; it's having the courage to show up and be seen." That moment of being seen—raw, real, and unfinished—is where shadow work and healing intersect. True connection begins where masks come off.

YESTERDAY: When were you most vulnerable in the past, and how did it shape you?

TODAY: In what areas of your life are you allowing yourself to be seen—messy, real, and whole?

TOMORROW: What would you risk showing the world if you no longer feared judgment?

The phrase "Living my best life" is often used to signal joy, abundance, and confidence. But behind the filter, it asks something deeper: What does a truly aligned life look like when no one's watching? What is your actual best life—not the performative one?

YESTERDAY: What did you once believe a "best life" looked like—and who taught you that?

TODAY: In what ways are you living a life that genuinely reflects your values?

TOMORROW: If you were living your most truthful, fulfilling life in five years—what would it look and feel like?

The nursery rhyme "Row, Row, Row Your Boat" sounds like a simple song—but it holds deep wisdom: "Life is but a dream." It invites us to flow, not force. To accept, not resist. And to find joy in the journey, even when we can't control the current.

YESTERDAY: When did you first learn to resist rather than flow? What shaped that approach to life?

TODAY: What would it look like to row gently in your life right now instead of paddling upstream?

TOMORROW: How can you embrace the idea that life is a dream—not to control, but to experience?

Robert's Rules of Order—a staple for structured meetings—includes a lesser-known rule: "No one may speak twice until all who wish to speak have spoken once." It's a guideline that prioritizes equality, patience, and intentional listening. What if we applied this rule not just in meetings—but in life?

YESTERDAY: When was a time your voice didn't get heard—or you didn't make space for someone else's?

TODAY: How do you balance speaking your truth with allowing others to be heard?

TOMORROW: What would life look like if your conversations—internal and external—honored both expression and silence?

The hymn "It Is Well with My Soul" is often sung in times of grief, acceptance, or surrender. It's not about everything being okay—it's about choosing inner peace even when the world isn't. That kind of peace doesn't come easily. It comes through hope, faith, and release.

YESTERDAY: Think of a time you had to find peace in the middle of pain. What helped carry you?

TODAY: What are you currently trying to make peace with, even if it still hurts?

TOMORROW: What would it look like to live with greater surrender—not through giving up, but by letting go?

In the *Twilight* series, Bella Swan is torn between two worlds—one familiar and safe, the other unknown and transformative. Her choice to walk into the unknown for love and identity represents a leap many of us face: choosing the path that feels deeper, darker, and far less certain—but somehow more honest.

YESTERDAY: When did you first choose something unconventional that others didn't understand? What drew you to it?

TODAY: What part of your life feels like it exists between two versions of yourself?

TOMORROW: What unknown are you willing to walk into if it means becoming more aligned with who you truly are?

"The Bare Necessities" from *The Jungle Book* reminds us to look for joy in simplicity. In a culture of striving, the idea of "forget about your worries and your strife" feels revolutionary. What truly sustains you isn't always more—but less.

YESTERDAY: What "necessities" brought you joy in childhood that you've forgotten now?

TODAY: What simple things nourish or ground you right now—emotionally, spiritually, or physically?

TOMORROW: What would it look like to re-prioritize ease, simplicity, and what really matters?

The phrase "I can do hard things" became a quiet battle cry for resilience—popularized by Glennon Doyle and others, yet rooted in a truth we've always known. It's not a declaration of ease. It's a statement of willingness.

YESTERDAY: When did you survive something you once believed you couldn't?

TODAY: What's one "hard thing" you're currently doing, even if it doesn't look heroic from the outside?

TOMORROW: What hard thing are you preparing yourself for—and how can you meet it with grace instead of fear?

In *The Breakfast Club*, five students walk into detention as strangers wearing labels—brain, athlete, basket case, princess, and criminal. By the end, they see each other (and themselves) in a new light. The film reminds us that identity isn't fixed—and connection requires vulnerability.

YESTERDAY: What label were you given growing up, and how did it shape your view of yourself?

TODAY: What part of your identity are you redefining or expanding?

TOMORROW: How can you continue to connect with others in ways that break down assumptions?

The phrase "We were on a break!" from the hit TV show *Friends* became a comedic lightning rod—but it's rooted in a deeper idea: misunderstandings, miscommunications, and the gray areas of relationships. Sometimes breaks aren't about time apart, but the distance we feel when we stop truly hearing each other.

YESTERDAY: Think of a time when you and someone important drifted—what created the disconnect?

TODAY: How do you currently handle relationship tension, space, or unspoken feelings?

TOMORROW: What relationship in your life deserves more clarity, repair, or reconnection?

In *Superbad*, the character Fogell confidently adopts the fake ID name "McLovin," creating an alternate persona to feel powerful and accepted. It's a humorous take on a serious truth: many of us live behind versions of ourselves we think are more likable, safer, or less rejected.

YESTERDAY: When did you last create a version of yourself to "fit in"? What were you afraid to reveal?

TODAY: What parts of your true self still feel hidden beneath a social persona?

TOMORROW: Who do you want to be when you no longer need a "McLovin" shield?

“And the award goes to…” is the iconic line that kicks off nearly every awards show—glamorous, dramatic, and filled with anticipation. But in real life, most of our deepest growth doesn’t come with applause or a shining trophy. We often do the hard, invisible work—healing, showing up, changing—and no one announces it. No standing ovation. Just quiet resilience. And yet, those are the moments that matter most.

YESTERDAY: Recall a time you gave your all—emotionally, mentally, or physically—and didn’t receive recognition. How did that affect you?

TODAY: Where in your life are you still showing up, even when no one sees it?

TOMORROW: How can you begin to honor your own progress, even without external validation?

The phrase "Don't bite the hand that feeds you" is a classic warning against betrayal or ingratitude—especially when someone supports you. But what happens when the hand that feeds you also holds you back? Sometimes, the support we receive comes with control, expectation, or strings attached.

YESTERDAY: When were you taught to stay loyal or silent out of obligation, even when it felt misaligned?

TODAY: What relationships or systems currently provide support—but at a cost to your autonomy?

TOMORROW: How can you express gratitude while still honoring your boundaries and values?

The Knights of the Round Table in Arthurian legend symbolized equality, honor, and shared purpose. There was no "head" of the table—just a circle of individuals bound by mission and loyalty. It raises the question: who sits at the table of your life, and are they helping or harming your quest?

YESTERDAY: Who in your past was part of your "round table"—your support system—and how did they shape your journey?

TODAY: Who do you currently surround yourself with, and do they reflect your values and growth?

TOMORROW: What kind of people do you want in your circle as you continue your quest toward a more whole version of yourself?

Smell-O-Vision was a 1960s invention that attempted to bring scent into movie theaters. Though it flopped, it represented a desire to experience life more vividly, more fully—through all senses. It reminds us that our memories, emotions, and healing are not just in our minds, but in the smells, sounds, and textures around us.

YESTERDAY: What scent instantly brings back a vivid memory from your past? What emotion is tied to it?

TODAY: What sensory experiences ground you in the present—smell, sound, taste, or touch?

TOMORROW: How can you create more sensory moments in your life that evoke peace, joy, or clarity?

Metallica's "Nothing Else Matters" is more than a rock ballad—it's a reminder to let go of others' expectations and follow your own truth. The line "I never opened myself this way… trust I seek and I find in you" is about vulnerability, trust, and what really matters when everything else is stripped away.

YESTERDAY: What did you once think mattered most, only to find it wasn't fulfilling?

TODAY: What do you genuinely value now—beyond appearances, status, or validation?

TOMORROW: If nothing else mattered except what's real, what would you devote yourself to?

The phrase "Use what you have" is both practical advice and a soulful challenge. It asks us to stop waiting until we feel ready, perfect, or better equipped—and to begin now. Whether it's a gift, a voice, or a story, what you have is already enough.

YESTERDAY: What have you overlooked in yourself that others saw as valuable?

TODAY: What do you already have—skills, experience, insight—that you're underestimating?

TOMORROW: What could you create or shift if you trusted in what's already in your hands?

Netflix's *Wednesday* series reimagined the iconic Addams Family daughter into a fiercely intelligent, emotionally complex anti-hero. Her story challenges the idea that darkness equals dysfunction—and that

YESTERDAY: What traits did others label as "too much," "too dark," or "too different" in you?

TODAY: How are you embracing your complexities—emotionally, creatively, or socially

TOMORROW: What version of yourself are you ready to fully step into, without apology?

In *Wicked*, the song "For Good" reflects on the deep impact people have on our lives—even if they don't stay. But the heart of Wicked is bigger than one song. It's a story about being misunderstood, rising in defiance, and realizing that being labeled "wicked" often says more about the world than it does about you. It's about the power of rewriting your narrative, even when others get it wrong.

YESTERDAY: Who misunderstood or misjudged you in the past—and how did that shape your identity?

TODAY: What version of your story are you currently rewriting or reclaiming?

TOMORROW: If you could show the world the real you—unfiltered, unedited—what would that look like, and what would you say?

In a world of constant connection, a digital detox can feel radical. We're encouraged to be online, on-brand, and always available—but stepping away from screens isn't just about silence. It's about reclaiming attention, presence, and self-worth from algorithms and noise. It's about remembering who you are without a feed.

YESTERDAY: When did you first realize your identity or self-worth was being shaped by digital validation?

TODAY: What role does technology currently play in your sense of peace, focus, or overstimulation?

TOMORROW: How can you create intentional space for stillness and presence in a hyper-connected world?

Rascal Flatts' "Bless the Broken Road" is a country anthem to detours. The lyrics tell the story of winding paths, heartbreaks, and wrong turns that eventually led somewhere meaningful. It's a song about hindsight, grace, and the idea that even the most painful chapters may have served a purpose.

YESTERDAY: What broken road have you walked that felt directionless at the time?

TODAY: What people, places, or experiences do you now see as essential—despite the pain they brought?

TOMORROW: How can you continue to trust the path, even when it looks nothing like you planned?

The Last of Us is more than a post-apocalyptic survival story—it's about love, trauma, and what we're willing to do to protect what matters. Joel and Ellie's journey forces us to confront the gray areas of loyalty, morality, and emotional walls built from loss. Sometimes, the real danger isn't outside—it's what we carry inside.

YESTERDAY: When did you last build emotional walls to protect yourself? What were you trying to survive?

TODAY: What part of your inner world still feels guarded or closed off?

TOMORROW: What might healing require—risking connection again, or finally facing what hurt you?

Wanderlust is more than a desire to travel—it's a pull toward freedom, discovery, and expansion. Sometimes it's about physical places. Other times, it's about emotional or spiritual movement: the restlessness we feel when our soul knows we've outgrown where we are.

YESTERDAY: When was the first time you felt the urge to break routine and go somewhere new—physically or emotionally?

TODAY: Where are you currently longing to go, and what do you think you'll find there?

TOMORROW: How can you build a life that allows for both rootedness and the freedom to roam?

Piccadilly®